INCREDIBLE YouTube RECORDS
AND FANTASTIC FEATS

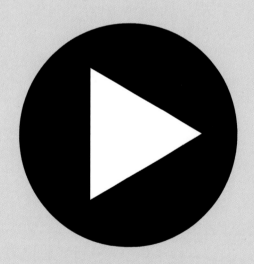

Amanda Harrison

STAYING SAFE
Many of the stunts and activities shown in this book involve significant risks and should not be attempted by children or anyone without proper training. The author and publisher are not responsible for any injuries, accidents, or harm resulting from attempting to recreate or perform any of the scenarios depicted in this book.

STAYING SAFE … ONLINE
The QR codes in this book link to videos on YouTube™ that have been carefully reviewed for appropriateness at the time of publication. However, due to the changing nature of the internet, the author and publisher cannot be held responsible for the content or availability of these videos. Nor are they responsible for any advertisements or comments that appear alongside these videos. We advise that children always be supervised when using the internet.

This edition published in 2025 by Arcturus Publishing Limited
26/27 Bickels Yard, 151–153 Bermondsey Street,
London SE1 3HA

Copyright © Arcturus Holdings Limited

All rights reserved. No part of this publication may be reproduced, stored in a retrieval system, or transmitted, in any form or by any means, electronic, mechanical, photocopying, recording, or otherwise, without prior written permission in accordance with the provisions of the Copyright Act 1956 (as amended). Any person or persons who do any unauthorized act in relation to this publication may be liable to criminal prosecution and civil claims for damages.

Author: Amanda Harrison
Designer: Lorraine Inglis
Picture research: Lorraine Inglis and Paul Futcher
Editor: Becca Clunes
Editorial assistant: Asha Francis
Design manager: Jessica Holliland
Managing editor: Joe Harris

ISBN: 978-1-3988-5636-3
CH012822NT
Supplier 13, Date 0425, PI 00009581

Printed in China

Picture credits

Alamy 10b (Frank Bienewald), 9tr, 14l, 21t, 23br, 68br (PA Images), 16l, 40L (Phil Taylor), 19bl, 59tr (dpa picture alliance), 19tr (Paul Swinney), 21b (Maximum Film), 22b, 33b, 38l, 38r, 39t, 44bl, 50br, 50l, 81tr, 86l (Associated Press), 22t (Richard Levine), 23bl (Lorenzo Dalberto), 25t (Tim Scrivener), 27t (AJ Pics), 34bl (Deborah Vernon), 35b (2ebill), 37b (Dorset Media Service), 43br (Julian Eales), 44r, 72-73cb, 87b (Abaca Press), 45br (Aflo Co. Ltd.), 45t (Sipa US), 49br (Imaginechina Limited), 51b (Jeff Morgan 02), 55tl (Steve Barnett), 67l (Ira Berger), 68l (frederic REGLAIN), 70r (NASA Photo), 76l (Tami Ruble), 81b (David Parker), 83t (Newscom), 89tl, 93tr (ZUMA Press, Inc.), 92l (WENN Rights Ltd), 94r (Hemis). **BMW AG** 18-19tc. **Emirates Team New Zealand** 77t. **Engineered Arts** 88b. **Getty** 8l (TANG CHHIN SOTHY/AFP), 18l (MediaNews Group/Boston Herald), 20tl (PATRICK LIN/AFP), 25b (Visual China Group), 31t (Lefty Shivambu/Gallo Images), 35tr (Hugh R Hastings), 46l (Valerio Pennicino), 51t (BOB MARTIN FOR OIS/IOC/AFP), 54b (Mlenny), 61t (Paul Harris), 63t (Hasan Mrad/UCG/Universal Images Group), 84r (Ksenia Kuleshova/Bloomberg), 87tr (PAU BARRENA/AFP). **Guinness World Records** 20b, 20b inset, 23t, 29cr, 29tr, 33t, 47t, 49t, 52cr, 52tr, 56b, 56t, 58l, 76tr, 85b, 8br, 90r, 91b (Courtesy of Guinness World Records Limited), 28bl (© 2023 RTI), 53bl, 58-59cc, 66b, 75tl, 79t, 85t (@ Guinness World Records Limited). **Jaan Parmask** 60l. **Jamescookartwork.com** 24l. **Joos Habraken** 14r. **Lorraine Inglis** 7cr, 24tr. **Mr. Lukas Pilz** 29bl, 44-45b. **Robert J. Lang** 6br, 15t. **Shutterstock** 4br (pics five), 4l, 82r (aiyoshi597), 4tr (Thais Ceneviva), 6tr, 10t (TSOMBOS Alexis), 6cr, 13b (Vepix), 6bl, 9b (YuniqueB), 6br, 15t (Anna Kondratiuk-Swiacka), 7bl (photo_vita_lina_byf), 7cl (Elena Eryomenko), 7tl, 17bl (BearFotos), 7tr (Evolf), 8-9ct (saiko3p), 11l (Ashley Whitworth), 11r (topten22photo), 12l (david muscroft), 12r (konstantin belovtov), 13t (Joshua Chew Visuals), 15b (Michael Warwick), 16br (Viktorya Telminova), 17r (Just Another Photographer), 17tc (in_colors), 18br (Natalia Mylova), 24br (Urbanscape), 26l (Pixel-Shot), 27b (Michael R Brown), 28br, 39b (kev Hughes), 28cl, 30t (ronstik), 28cr, 36tr (Tatiana Popova), 28tr, 34-35t (Billion Photos), 29br, 50-51t (Christian Weber), 29cl, 43t (Alex Bogatyrev), 29tl, 40-41ct (1000 Words), 30b (vectorfusionart), 31b (Sergei Bachlakov), 32l (Joma_JOMANOX), 32r (EA Given), 34br (vhpicstock), 36br (Dragon Images), 36l (Focus Pix), 37t (Celso Pupo), 40-41bc (KOMTHONG-APEC), 40bl (PNPImages), 41tr (Ilya Images), 42-43b (Pratiksha _h), 42l (Ruslan Huzau), 46r (Martin Charles Hatch), 47b (Andy Soloman), 48l (Flystock), 48r (Alex Brylov), 49bl (Greg and Jan Ritchie), 52bl, 54t (PaPicasso), 52br, 61b (proslgn), 53br, 72-73ct (Capturing Adventure), 53cr, 71b (nicemyphoto), 53tl, 63b (marekuliasz), 53tr, 68br (Peter Cowles), 55bl (Vitalii Hulai), 55bl (MakroBetz), 55bl (New Africa), 55r (Pavel1964), 56b (Elena_E), 57r (Tamara Kulikova), 58br (Nicky Rhodes), 59b (Bigzumi), 5b (Mix Tape), 5t (Jacek Chabraszewski), 60br (CCISUL), 60cr (Alexandre.ROSA), 62l (EugeneEdge), 62r (YueStock), 64-65ct (silvae), 64br (Danita Delimont), 53cl, 65b (Viktorishy), 66t (Protasov AN), 67br (PaulSat), 67tr (Jeff Whyte), 68-69ct (Thorir Ingvarsson), 69b (mobrafotografie), 69tr (Benoit Daoust), 70l (YANGYANG FANG), 71t (Susan B Sheldon), 72l (Mario Chipev), 73r (hurricanehank), 74bl, 76-77bc (cristiano barni), 74br, 83b (Jenson), 74cr, 80-81tc (Daniele Gambitta), 74tr, 79b (Olena Yakobchuk), 75bl, 88t (Scharfsinn), 75br, 95b (FooTToo), 75cl, 86-87tc (RavenaJuly), 75cr, 93br (AP17), 75tr, 91t (Daniyal Ali Butt), 78l (Kaspars Grinvalds), 78r (Andrew Harker), 80br (Kzenon), 80l (Artsiom P), 82l (Sheviakova Kateryna), 82r (aiyoshi597), 84l (IndustryAndTravel), 89bl (Fierman Much), 89r (Lukas Kovarik), 90l (Studio Romantic), 92-93tc (Balate.Dorin), 94l (reddees), 95t (Zhuravlev Andrey). **Wikimedia Commons** 7br, 26r (Stefan Brending), 42tr (WCBO), 57l (JJRam86), 64l (steffen), 92-93bc (Vertiflite).

CONTENTS

Introduction	4
Chapter 1: Cool Culture	**6**
Mega Art	8
Animal Festivals	10
Dazzling Dress Up	12
Inspired by Nature	14
Food Festivals	16
Original Orchestras	18
Microscopic Makers	20
Food Art	22
Tech Art	24
Surprising Sounds	26
Chapter 2: Above and Beyond	**28**
Ball Games for All	30
Dancing with a Difference	32
Extraordinary Events	34
Fastest Feats	36
Flying High	38
Eat or Compete?	40
Grown-up Games	42
Jeopardous Jumps	44
Wheeled Wonders	46
Up High	48
Wins on Water	50
Chapter 3: Extraordinary Everyday	**52**
Ready, Set, Run!	54
Cool Clothes	56
Performing Pets	58
Home Sweet Home	60
Tough Trips	62
Spectacular Stays	64
Colossal Collections	66
What a Job!	68
Unforgettable Food	70
Hazardous Hobbies	72
Chapter 4: Top Tech	**74**
Let's Go Fast!	76
Awe-inspiring Inventions	78
Mini Mechanics	80
Robots Assemble	82
Mighty Machines	84
Inspiring Inventions	86
Helping Hand	88
Long and Strong	90
People Power	92
Ridiculous Rides	94
Index	96

HOW TO USE THIS BOOK

There are many QR codes in this book—they look like the red square on the right. If you want to watch a video relating to a particular fact, simply open the camera app on your phone or tablet and point it at the code. Hold the device still until a link appears, then tap on that link. You will be taken straight to the relevant YouTube™ video!

4 | INTRODUCTION

INTRODUCTION

Welcome to a whistle-stop tour of some of the most brilliant—and most bonkers—feats and records you'll find on YouTube™ today. From astronomically priced art to subzero sprints, this book will have you gasping at the amazing things people have achieved. And maybe it will inspire you to achieve an awe-inspiring feat of your own!

   SHARE

What is YouTube™?

Of course you've heard of YouTube™—it's the video-sharing website where you can find something to watch on almost any subject in the world! It's a great resource to learn a new skill, find information about a subject, or—just like in this book—watch some amazing people perform mind-boggling stunts!

Be Safe on the Internet

YouTube™ is an awesome tool, but you should be smart about how you use it. Make sure the adults in your life know what content you're viewing—and that you have their permission. Always follow the rules set by your family around internet usage. For example, stay on the website you've said you want to use and never share any personal information. When in doubt, talk to a responsible adult about your online activities.

THE SKY'S THE LIMIT!

INTRODUCTION | 5

Don't try EVERYTHING in this Book at Home

Of course, you might want to have a go at breaking a record yourself, but please check in with a responsible adult first! Trying to speedily solve a Rubik's cube poses little risk, other than achy fingers... but zooming down the tallest hill you can find without considering the safety of yourself or others first may not work out as you expect it to. Many of the people in this book have made their stunts super-safe and are often working with whole teams of people to consider every possible outcome. So don't be silly—speak to your grown-up and be safe!

 SAFETY FIRST!

How to be a Stunt Superstar

Here are three things to consider if you're inspired to set a record:

1. What are you good at already?
   - Keepy uppies—how many can you do in a minute? Could you do it with one eye closed? Or while hopping on one leg?
   - Drawing—could you draw something really big or really small? What about using a new material to draw with or draw on?
   - Arithmetic—how many sums can you solve in a minute? Can you do it with or without paper? What about dealing with bigger numbers?

2. Practice, practice, and practice some more! The feats in this book were not achieved in one day. Write down your goal, and then document your progress on your first attempt, and again on your 10th, 20th, and so on. This allows you to see your improvement over time and know your goal is in sight.

3. Once you're happy with what you can do, ask your grown-up to help you record a video. Watch it back and take a moment to feel proud of what you've achieved! If your grown-up says it's OK, share the video with friends and family.

DON'T STOP!

TOP PICK!

CHAPTER 1

COOL CULTURE

Find out about some of the most amazing and innovative music, art, and events from around the world!

: Animal Festivals

Celebrate our best buddies like never before!

PAGE 10

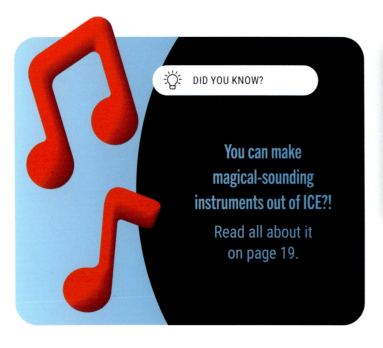

💡 **DID YOU KNOW?**

You can make magical-sounding instruments out of ICE?!

Read all about it on page 19.

: Dazzling Dress Up

Discover creative costumes that make a statement.

PAGE 12

: Mega Art

Marvel at spectacular art on a massive scale.

PAGE 8

: Inspired by Nature

From dinosaurs to birds, this is nature art gone wild.

PAGE 14

: Food Festivals

Find out about foodie festivals and fruity fights.

PAGE 16

: Food Art

This food art is striking, creative, and delicious!

PAGE 22

: Original Orchestras

From typewriters to veggies, this music is truly unique.

PAGE 18

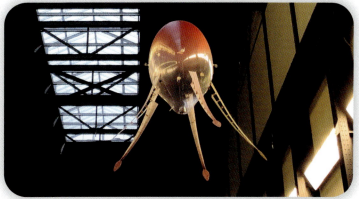

: Tech Art

See how robots can make something beautiful.

PAGE 24

: Microscopic Makers

Art small enough to fit in the eye of a needle!

PAGE 20

: Surprising Sounds

Discover some unexpected sound-makers.

PAGE 26

CHAPTER 1: Cool Culture

MEGA ART

Artists around the world often use their work to share a message—and the bigger the art, the louder the message! To make art on such a grand scale, artists need to choose the right materials and exhibit extraordinary skill.

Giant Gorilla

Cambodian artist Mean Tithpheap has spent four years creating magnificent, giant sculptures out of old rubber. His goal is to demonstrate that something great can be made from waste. He used 500 bicycle and motorcycle wheels to make a 2.5-m/8-ft tall King Kong-like gorilla in a field in Phnom Penh in Cambodia. It took him more than five weeks to make.

ROAR!

Mocha Masterpiece

Sree Raj Santhappan, from India, has created the largest painting using coffee in the world. The huge portrait (325 sq m/3,500 sq ft) portrait shows Queen Elizabeth II, in multiple shades of brown. Sree is completely self-taught. He simply followed his dream of being a painter—and this mega creation awarded him a world record!

CHAPTER 1: Cool Culture | 9

Jumbo Ride

If you visit Nantes, France, you may see this huge mechanical elephant lumbering around. It can fit up to 50 passengers inside its belly for a walking tour. Standing at 12 m (39 ft) tall, the beast is made of steel and wood. It even blasts water from its trunk!

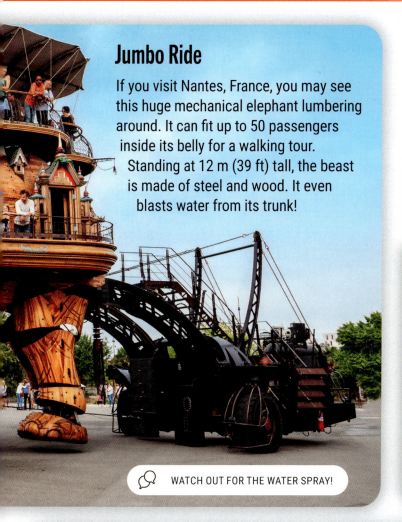

WATCH OUT FOR THE WATER SPRAY!

Huge Head

Could you create a giant, lifelike human or animal from card? James Lake can! James starts each large 3D sculpture by designing lots of detailed individual pieces, which are then slotted together like a giant jigsaw puzzle. Finally, each piece is coated in a special hardener to stop any accidental water damage destroying his hard work!

Cadillac Creation

Fancy designing a motor masterpiece?

Driving along the road in Amarillo, Texas, you might be surprised to come across 10 Cadillac cars standing tall, with their noses buried in the ground. This awesome installation was created in 1974 to celebrate the Cadillac. Passersby are invited to stop and add to the creation using cans of spray paint.

SEE PAGE 87 FOR A CAR THAT'S TOTALLY BANANAS!

ANIMAL FESTIVALS

To celebrate our prized animal companions and wonderful wild animals, we humans put on extravagant festivals and events all around the world. Some of the celebrated animals are even treated to banquets of food fit for royalty!

Frog Festivities

During heatwaves in India, where temperatures reach 45 °C (113 °F), people reach out to the God of Rain, Indra, to bring a downpour—by hosting a lavish wedding between two frogs! The frogs are dressed in special outfits and driven through the streets. They may even be given wedding bands for their toes.

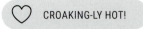

Fish Funeral

Each spring, in the Spanish city of Murcia, you can join in the huge, three-day-long fish funeral. Named the Burial of the Sardine, the festival includes an elaborate carnival, a sardine mascot who entertains the crowds, and a fireworks finale with the burning of a giant papier mâché sardine!

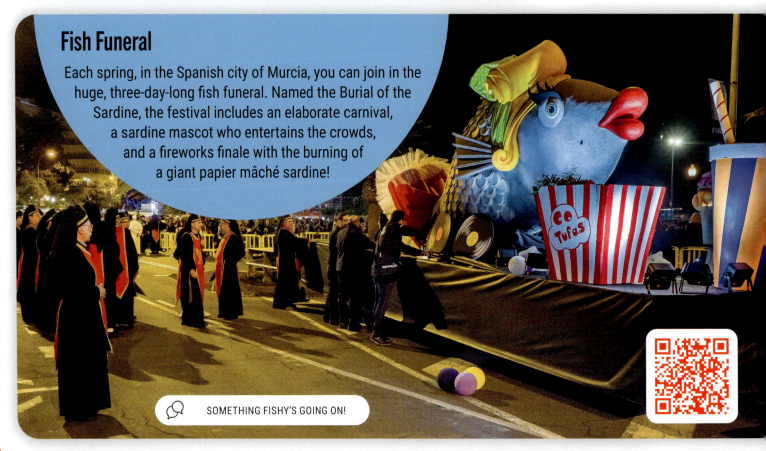

CHAPTER 1: Cool Culture | 11

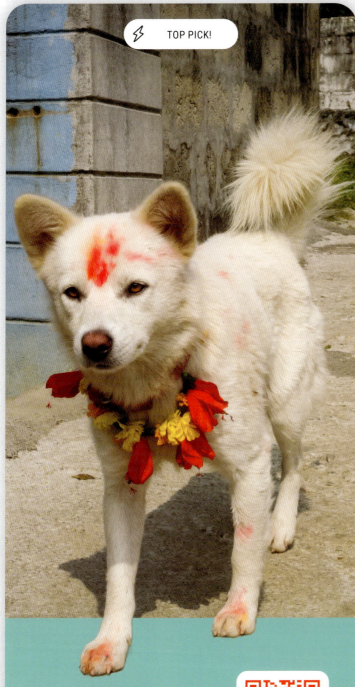

TOP PICK!

Day of the Dogs

The second day of the Hindu festival of Tihar is dedicated to celebrating pooches! Dogs—both pets and strays—are given a flower garland, a red mark on their head called a *tika*, and plenty of good food. This special day is to thank our canine chums for their friendship, loyalty, and love.

SHARE

Monkey Meals

At the end of November, in Lopburi, Thailand, people gather huge quantities of fruit and vegetables for a fantastic feast—for monkeys! It's a tasty way to thank the 4,000 local macaques for attracting so many tourists to the area. Cherries and blueberries seem to be the food the monkeys like best.

TASTY TREAT!

MORE FEASTS ON PAGE 70!

12 | CHAPTER 1: Cool Culture

DAZZLING DRESS UP

Parades and festivals are made even more memorable by the creative costumes people wear. Some attire is traditional to remember local cultures and customs. Some get-ups are flamboyant to celebrate vitality and fun!

 SHARE

Straw Suit

Every January, in Whittlesey, England, a giant bear made of straw leads a procession! The straw bear costume weighs a hefty 32 kg (70 lb) and is worn for the entire parade. More than 250 dancers, musicians, and performers take part. The tradition is believed to have once celebrated farmers returning to work.

MORE CRAZY COSTUMES ON PAGE 56!

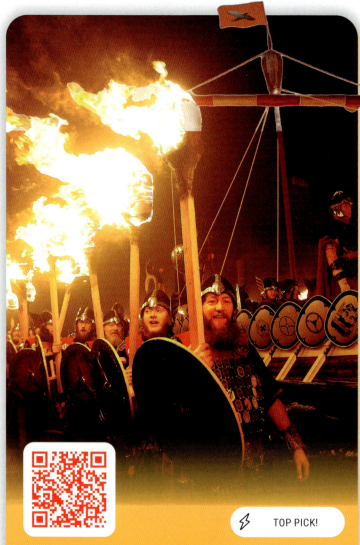

TOP PICK!

Viking Style

The Norse festival of Up Helly Aa is celebrated each January in Shetland, Scotland. After a day of festivities, the grand finale is a torchlit procession through the streets by 1,000 participants dressed as Viking warriors. Finally, as they reach the Viking longship, the "warriors" toss their flaming torches onto it, watching the ship burn to ashes!

CHAPTER 1: **Cool Culture** | 13

Flower Fashion

The Panagbenga Flower Festival in the Philippines sees participants dress up as magnificent flowers! The month-long celebration in February includes elaborate parades, street dances, and a grand fireworks display—all to celebrate the city's flowers as they come into bloom.

FANTASTIC FLORAL FESTIVITIES!

Canal Clauses

The city of Venice, Italy, hosts a Christmas Regatta each December. One of the highlights is seeing a sea of Santas run through the streets before jumping into festively decorated gondolas and rowing along Venice Grand Canal, waving to onlookers.

HO, HO, HO!

14 | CHAPTER 1: Cool Culture

INSPIRED BY NATURE

Who needs to buy art supplies from a store? These inventive artists use the natural world to create their masterpieces. First, they find their inspiration in nature. Then, they create art within nature's conditions and time limits, using materials they discover on any given day.

CARCASS CREATIONS

Meet reimagined insect warriors!

Artist Joos Habraken creates 15-cm/6-in tall soldier sculptures, each made with up to 100 body parts of 30 different insects. He makes dresses out of wings, hair out of legs, and archery bows out of antennae. But Joos only uses bugs that have already died—he never kills wild creatures to make art.

: Dinosaur Designs

Forget finding dinosaur fossils. Artist David Popa has gone one better and created a large-scale dinosaur mural on rock! With ice or stone as his canvas, David uses natural pigments, chalk, and charcoal to quickly create his prehistoric pictures before the weather changes and washes it all away.

MORE INCREDIBLE ART ON PAGE 24!

CHAPTER 1: **Cool Culture** | 15

Out-of-this-World Origami

Former NASA engineer Robert Lang uses both his mathematical training and his keen interest in nature to come up with complex origami models—some have up to 1,000 steps! As well as designing animals out of both paper and stainless steel, he supported NASA in developing a giant shade that folded up to fit inside a rocket.

UNFOLDING SOME GREAT DESIGNS!

Sand Sketches

After years of working as a doctor, Claire Eason, who lives near Northumberland, UK, discovered that she had a talent for creating giant murals in sand. Starting at low tide, she uses a garden rake to create magnificent images, with each taking up to four hours to create. Her previous artworks include a sea serpent, an owl, a surfer, and even a nativity scene!

TOP PICK!

FOOD FESTIVALS

Food is a necessity of human life, so it is greatly celebrated, but not always in ways you'd imagine! From epic food fights to peculiar parades, event organizers around the world serve up some strange and surprising food festivals!

Sausage Slinging

Hundreds of people gather in Bury, UK, to see competitors take part in an unusual food competition—they throw black pudding sausages at a pile of batter puddings to see how many they can knock down! The silly shenanigan raises money for local charities.

PUMPKIN PARTY!

From August to November, Ludwigsburg in southwest Germany hosts a pumpkin festival, celebrating this wonderful squash with 450,000 pumpkins of 600 different varieties! Elaborate sculptures and carved creations decorate the site, and competitive growers take part in the European Giant Pumpkin Weigh-Off, with the heaviest weighing in at more than 1,150 kg (2,535 lb). That's heavier than a small car!

Pickle Parade

Every July, Pittsburgh, Pennsylvania, US, hosts Picklesburgh: a four-day festival where EVERYTHING, from food to clothing, is related to pickles. Daring visitors can try unusual foods such as pickled cheese popcorn, pickle beer, and chocolate-covered pickles—or take part in a competition to drink a jar of pickle juice in just a few seconds!

CHAPTER 1: Cool Culture | 17

TOP PICK!

Tomato Tussle

The world-famous Tomatina Festival in Spain brings a whole new meaning to "food fight." For one hour, in the town's main square, 22,000 participants throw 160 tonnes (176 tons) of tomatoes at each other. When the hour is up, a rocket is fired, the fight is over, and the colossal clean-up begins.

Radish Revelry

The Night of the Radishes festival began in Oaxaca, Mexico, during the 16th century, to celebrate the new vegetable. Every year, artists carve oversized radishes into unique sculptures, which are put on display the evening of the festival.

LOOKING RADISHING!

MORE FUN WITH FOOD ON PAGE 40!

18 | CHAPTER 1: Cool Culture

ORIGINAL ORCHESTRAS

Can absolutely any sound be music? Some musicians seem to think so—and they've invented incredibly innovative instruments to prove their point! From using everyday vegetables to intricate ice carvings, these original-sounding orchestras make it their mission to entertain in unique ways.

 SHARE

Typewriter Tunes

The Boston Typewriter Orchestra plays songs at national events and festivals, using 70-year-old typewriters as instruments! They can create a whole range of sounds by tapping keys, ringing bells, and thumping the casing onto tables. But each typewriter instrument lasts for only two years!

TRY HITTING THE RIGHT NOTE!

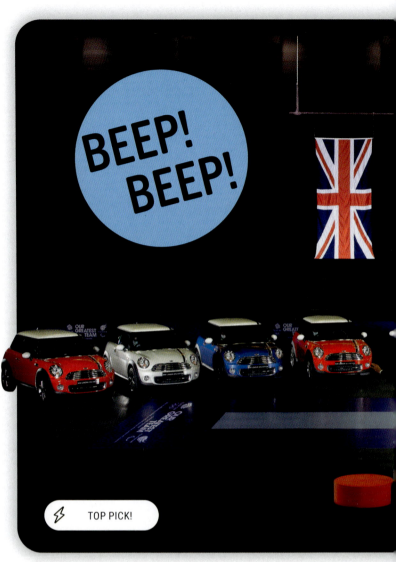

BEEP! BEEP!

⚡ TOP PICK!

Veggie Vibrations

Do you fancy soup or sound?

The Vienna Vegetable Orchestra makes instruments out of all kinds of vegetables, including onions, carrots, and squash. Each vegetable instrument is crafted using knives and drills, or used just as it is in the case of dry onion skins. Any unused vegetables are made into soup to share with the audience after the show!

CHAPTER 1: **Cool Culture** | 19

Unusual Horns

To celebrate the Queen's Jubilee, the London Philharmonic Orchestra chose some unusual instruments to play the national anthem: nine special edition MINI cars! Each car was fitted with a different-sounding horn, so the nine musicians could play the correct notes.

⚡ TOP PICK!

Ice Instruments

American ice sculptor Tim Linhart has built hundreds of ice instruments since his first octobass in 1998. Since then, he's developed ways to stop the instruments from melting or exploding. Audiences can attend concerts in his custom-built concert igloos, with seating for up to 300 people.

♡ BRRR-ILLIANT CONCERTS! 👍

20 | CHAPTER 1: Cool Culture

MICROSCOPIC MAKERS

Art can be made and shown in many sizes, including really, really small—microscopic, in fact! These innovative artists not only create incredible art on the smallest scale, but they also invent tools that deliver the smallest paint strokes or sculpture scrapes.

TOP PICK!

Pilau Painting

Self-taught artist Chen Forng-Shean paints detailed pictures onto the smallest, most challenging canvas he can find—grains of rice! Using a magnifying glass, he carefully controls both his breath and movement, before applying each stroke with a hair-thin paintbrush.

SHARE

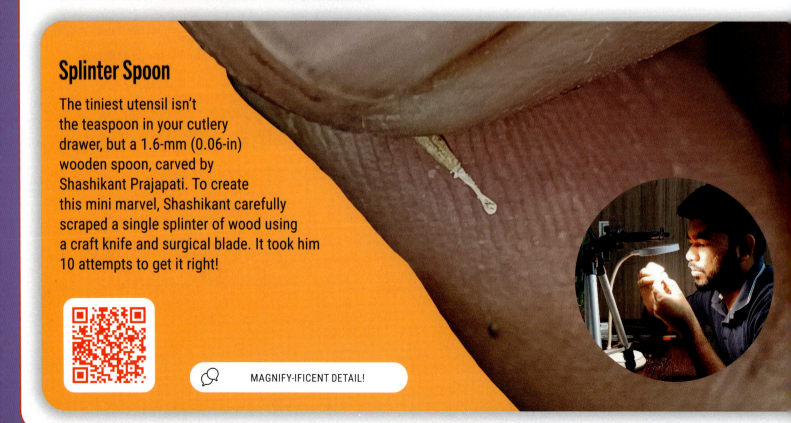

Splinter Spoon

The tiniest utensil isn't the teaspoon in your cutlery drawer, but a 1.6-mm (0.06-in) wooden spoon, carved by Shashikant Prajapati. To create this mini marvel, Shashikant carefully scraped a single splinter of wood using a craft knife and surgical blade. It took him 10 attempts to get it right!

MAGNIFY-IFICENT DETAIL!

CHAPTER 1: **Cool Culture** | 21

SMALLEST SCULPTURES

The first teeny things Willard Wigan ever made were chairs and a table for the ants in his yard—he was just five years old! He now makes delicate, detailed sculptures—from Einstein to Little Red Riding Hood—that fit into the eye of a needle. His tools include paintbrushes made from eyelashes and dog hair, spiderweb glue, and a diamond-splinter chisel!

💬 YOU'LL NEED A STEADY HAND FOR THIS!

Mini Movie Set

Film sets in miniature!

Hobbyist Bridget McCarty builds famous film and TV sets out of wood, paper, and glue! Inspired by her grandmother who loved tiny objects, Bridget can spend up to a month on a complicated scene. The scenes are super realistic because she pays attention to the details, such as the bedposts, shelf brackets, and mobile in this scene from *Monsters, Inc.*

FOOD ART

Art can be created from almost anything, including, believe it or not, foodstuffs! And some art is even made to look like food—to be recognizable and relatable to art lovers and curious viewers alike.

Felt Food

Artist Lucy Sparrow hand-made a whole supermarket out of felt, including 31,000 items, shelving, and signs. This felty feat took Lucy and five team members a year to complete, and then a few days to set up the Sparrow Market where customers could buy every product for £4–60 ($5–75).

FROZEN OR FELT?!

Is it Cake?

Tuba Geckil is the founder of a cake studio in Istanbul, and she has a rather unique talent—she can make ultra-realistic cakes. Each bake takes between two hours and two days to put together. She uses sponge, frosting, and edible paint for her creations, which include phones, shoes, and full-sized celebrity figures.

THE ICING ON THE CAKE!

CHAPTER 1: Cool Culture | 23

Cheese Creator

Artist Sarah Kaufmann is known as "The Cheese Lady" because she has carved more than 4,000 sculptures out of this dairy delight! Cheddar is her preferred cheese to work with because it holds its shape and comes in gigantic wheels. Her largest sculptures include an alligator, an astronaut, and a dragon!

 SHARE

Deluxe Decay

At first glance, Kathleen Ryan's art looks like oversized rotten fruit. But on closer inspection, the truth reveals itself. The "decay" is made of patterns of gemstones, such as opal, quartz, and malachite, interwoven with each fruit's skin of glass beads and pearls.

Pumpkin Portraits

Farm manager David Finkle took up pumpkin carving at a local competition and discovered he had a hidden talent. His lifelike celebrity portraits soon began to go viral. Most carvings take three to four hours of carving, but Dave went on to set a world record for the fastest face carving—in just 20 seconds!

 A CUT ABOVE THE REST!

24 | CHAPTER 1: Cool Culture

TECH ART

Technology is changing every aspect of the world around us—and the world of art is no exception. Artists are constantly finding new ways to use machines in their work, whether they are harnessing technology as a fun and unusual way to create traditional art, or incorporating new hardware into innovative artworks.

Symbol Scenes

Artist James Cook uses unusual tools to create his pictures: vintage typewriters. Each picture is made up of thousands of letters, numbers, and punctuation marks, to create different shades and textures. Each piece of paper goes through his typewriter thousands of times, building the incredible image in layers.

Ocean in the Air

Imagine seeing jellyfish floating in the air—it became a reality at London's Tate Modern gallery with Anicka Yi's helium-filled, robotic aerobes. The aerobes have been programmed to respond to the space around them, so they avoid obstacles and are drawn to human heat.

CHAPTER 1: **Cool Culture** | 25

Remote-controlled Craft

Forget paintbrushes—Ian Cook not only uses toy car wheels to paint with, but he's thrown in the added challenge of controlling them using a remote! To create an artwork, he splatters paint where needed, then uses different-sized cars to spread the paint and form the shapes he wants to create.

SPLAT!

MORE FUN AND GAMES ON PAGE 42!

AI Art

If you were to visit an exhibition of Agnieszka Pilat's work, you'd experience art being created before your very eyes by the three robotic dogs she has trained! The Boston Dynamic Robot Dogs don't follow an exact plan. Instead, they use AI to decide on how to paint their canvases.

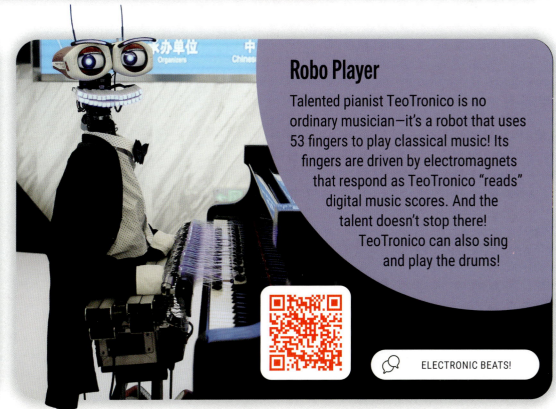

Robo Player

Talented pianist TeoTronico is no ordinary musician—it's a robot that uses 53 fingers to play classical music! Its fingers are driven by electromagnets that respond as TeoTronico "reads" digital music scores. And the talent doesn't stop there! TeoTronico can also sing and play the drums!

ELECTRONIC BEATS!

CHAPTER 1: Cool Culture

SURPRISING SOUNDS

The world is full of talented people performing amazing music and sounds to delight audiences, whether they're behind-the-scenes sound makers—such as voice actors—or up-front entertainers—such as stage musicians.

Shrinking Violins

How small can he play?

Classically trained violinist Rob Landes wants to change the way new generations think of classical music, so he uses YouTube™ to showcase modern music in a classical format. He even performs silly stunts—like playing the same piece on smaller and smaller violins—to entertain his audience.

Fantastic French Hornist

German French horn player Felix Klieser had his first lesson at only four years old. His exceptional talent led him to become part of the Royal Scottish National Orchestra. Remarkably, Felix presses the horn's valves with his left foot because he was born with no arms.

TOP PICK!

CHAPTER 1: **Cool Culture** | 27

Vault of Voices

Actor Dee Bradley Baker is the voice of hundreds of characters and animals from TV shows and films, including roles in *SpongeBob SquarePants* and *Space Jam*. He creates a backstory for each character so that he can not only give them the right voice, but also recall each character and switch between them easily.

Stalacpipe Sounds

The world's largest musical instrument is situated in Luray Caverns in Virginia, US. When a key is pressed on the Great Stalacpipe Organ, an electrical signal passes to a rubber mallet, which strikes one of 37 stalactites to make a sound. Even though the stalactites are spread over a massive 1.4 hectares (3.5 acres), the music can be heard anywhere in the caverns!

STAY TUNED!

CHAPTER 2

ABOVE AND BEYOND

Get ready to meet some of the fastest, fittest, and most fearless people on the planet!

Extraordinary Events

Competitions, from worm whispering to toe wrestling.

PAGE 34

Ball Games for All

Find out about ball games that are unique and fun.

PAGE 30

Fastest Feats

See sprinting, skipping, and solving at super speeds.

PAGE 36

Dancing with a Difference

Enjoy spectacular and unusual styles of dance.

PAGE 32

Flying High

From skydiving to sky skating, these fliers are fearless.

PAGE 38

: Eat or Compete?
Tuck in to these tasty food competitions!

PAGE 40

: Wheeled Wonders
Learn about stunts on mororbikes and mowers!

PAGE 46

: Grown-up Games
Watch grown-ups take kids' games to the next level.

PAGE 42

: Up High
Discover dramatic displays at death-defying heights!

PAGE 48

: Jeopardous Jumps
Enjoy extreme athletes performing super-high jumps.

PAGE 44

: Wins on Water
Check out the thrills—and spills—of water sports!

PAGE 50

30 | CHAPTER 2: Above and Beyond

BALL GAMES FOR ALL

Some modern ball games are less about traditional wins and, instead, promote the inclusion of all people so they can nurture and show off special skills—or just have fun! No matter your age, location, or fitness level, there's a ball game out there for you.

SHARE

Snooker Star

James Silverwood wanted to become a professional snooker player. When it didn't happen for him, he set his sights on a new goal. James trained every day until he could clear a snooker table in just 17 seconds, earning himself a place in the record books.

Strike and Sprint

British Open Speedgolf combines the precision of golf with the speed of running. With no time to ponder which club to try or stroke to use, speedgolfers must complete 18 holes around a 5-km (3-mi) course as fast as possible. Contestants aim to complete the course in under 30 minutes!

EACH HOLE IN UNDER TWO MINUTES—GO!

CHAPTER 2: **Above and Beyond** | 31

Grannies' Game

In South Africa, a group of women aged 55 years and older formed a soccer league that now includes more than 15 teams! The Grannies International Football Tournament gives the older generation a way to have fun, make friends, and stay healthy.

BRING ON THE CHEERLEADERS! SEE PAGE 83.

SIRIUS-LY GOOD FUN!

TOP PICK!

Real-life Quidditch

Around the world, from Belgium to Uganda, young people are taking up quadball: a game based on quidditch from the Harry Potter books! There are seven people on each team, each straddling a broomstick. There are three chasers who try to score, two beaters who defend the goal, a keeper, and a seeker who chases the "snitch." Instead of a flying golden ball, the snitch in this game is a yellow tennis ball attached to the back of a runner's shorts.

32 | CHAPTER 2: Above and Beyond

DANCING WITH A DIFFERENCE

Dedicated dancers around the world put on the most stunning spectacles for all to see, demonstrating their skill, precision, and commitment to their art. Some even overcome physical challenges or self-imposed jeopardy to give the performance of a lifetime!

Daring Display

The Dance of the Flyers is a Mexican tradition that began 600 years ago. It involves four "flyers," each tying one ankle to the top of a 20-m (65-ft) pole with a rope. Once in position, a fifth person plays a flute, to which the flyers perform an upside-down dance as though they are soaring through the sky!

Stilt Strollers

In Trinidad and Tobago, talented dancers are doing things differently—atop 3 m/10 ft-high, brightly decorated stilts! Moko Jumbies are traditional stilt walkers who perform special dance moves at celebrations and festivals. Training starts on much smaller stilts, so any falls aren't so painful!

CHAPTER 2: **Above and Beyond** | 33

SPINNING SHOW

DON'T GET TOO DIZZY!

Bianca Ciocirlan was only 10 years old when she had to stop figure skating after a knee injury. Undeterred, she took up the hoverboard to let her move without straining her knee. Now she performs shows full of dazzling dance moves and perfect pirouettes!

Pulsating Performance

The Disabled People's Performing Arts Troupe from China performs spectacular inclusive shows. The dancers, who are deaf, feel the vibrations of the music played by visually impaired musicians. Performing around the world, the 40-strong group spend as much time together as possible to strengthen their on-stage bond.

34 | CHAPTER 2: Above and Beyond

EXTRAORDINARY EVENTS

Not all feats feature extreme situations or physical prowess—some are just fresh and fun! If you have a mega moustache or you're an air guitar champion, there's a place for you in the Extraordinary Hall of Fame!

  SHARE

TOP PICK!

 TOE-TALLY AWESOME!

Ready, Steady, Toe

There are few competitions where the feet are inspected for infections before participants can begin—but the World Toe Wrestling Championship is one of them! Two competitors sit facing each other, lock toes, and then try to push their opponent's foot into the mini arena's sidewall.

MORE WRESTLING ON PAGE 40!

Brilliant Beards

Every two years, hairy rivals take part in the World Beard and Moustache Championships, showing off their fantastic facial creations. Participants may use wax and hairspray, but no dyes, extensions, or pins. There are 37 categories, including imperial moustache, business beard, and freestyle.

CHAPTER 2: **Above and Beyond** | 35

Guitar Gurus

Get your groove on!

To win the Air Guitar World Championships, performers take to the stage for a wild 60-second show, making the invisible guitar seem visible. They're judged on stage presence, artistic impression, and technical ability—hitting the right notes at the right time is crucial!

Worm Whisperers

In the World Worm Charming Championship, each group is given a plot of grass 2 sq m (21 sq ft) and 30 minutes to coax worms up from the ground! People stamp, sing, and play music to encourage the worms to pop up their heads.

Coal Carriers

Every year, hundreds of contestants motivate their muscles to take part in Yorkshire's World Coal Carrying Championship. Each man carries a 50-kg (100-lb) bag of coal on their back, and each woman carries a 20-kg (44-lb) bag, for a distance of 1,012 m (3,320 ft). The fastest time is just 4 minutes and 22 seconds!

MORE CRAZY COMPETITIONS ON PAGE 54!

36 | CHAPTER 2: Above and Beyond

FASTEST FEATS

With lots of practice, fierce determination, and a generous sprinkling of talent, some people are physically or mentally fast—whether they are running a race or completing mind-boggling puzzles.

  SHARE

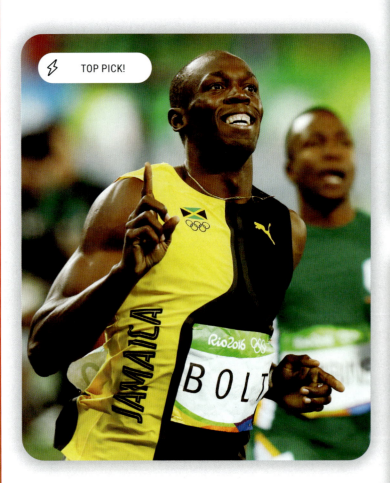

TOP PICK!

: Lightning Bolt

Jamaican sprinter Usain Bolt is officially the fastest man in the world! He has eight Olympic Gold medals for winning 100 m, 200 m, and 100 m relay races. No one has yet been able to beat his 2009 record of running 100 m (328 ft) in just 9.58 seconds!

MORE ATHLETES ON PAGE 44!

Rapid Rubik's

The Rubik's Cube was invented in 1974 by Erno Rubik and has gone on to be one of the most popular games around. And the fastest fingers to solve the cube conundrum take part in the competitive sport of Speedcubing. Max Park from California can solve a mixed-up 3×3×3 Rubik's Cube in just 3.13 seconds!

Swift Skipping

Three Nigerian students made it their mission to become the world's fastest rope skippers! Between them, they smashed six world records, including the most criss-crosses in 30 seconds and the most skips on one leg in 60 seconds!

CHAPTER 2: Above and Beyond | 37

Speedy Sprint

Sprinter David Brown was the first blind athlete to run 100 m (328 ft) in under 11 seconds—thanks to the guidance of his running partner Jerome Avery. The runners are connected by a short tether attached to their wrists, enabling them to run almost like they're one person.

Zippy Zip Line

Above a slate quarry sits the fastest zip line in the world. Zooming along the 1,500 m/ 4,920 ft-long zip line, thrill seekers can reach a speed of 160 km/h (100 mph) while taking in the magnificent views of the Welsh countryside—just as 85-year-old Sally Webster experienced when she checked it off her bucket list!

WHEEE!

CHAPTER 2: Above and Beyond

FLYING HIGH

Imagine jumping out of a helicopter wearing just a webbed jumpsuit, performing bike stunts in the sky, or steadily soaring a plane through a tunnel ... meet the fearless folk who did just that and more, all in a day's work!

SHARE

Super Skydive

Professional skydivers Marco Fürst and Marco Waltenspiel jumped out of a helicopter and used their wingsuits to glide through Tower Bridge in London. It took just 45 seconds from the jump to their parachute landing—and they reached a speed of 246 km/h (153 mph)!

TOP PICK!

Skate Park in the Sky

BMX rider Kriss Kyle took on the ultimate challenge when he performed stunts on a floating skate park! Suspended by a hot air balloon 610 m (2,000 ft) above the ground, the ramp swung from side to side, making the skate tricks even more challenging to complete!

CHAPTER 2: Above and Beyond | 39

Fearless Flight

Stunt pilot Dario Costa is the first person to ever fly a small plane through a tunnel. With a steady hand and nerves of steel, he guided the plane through two tunnels—with the wingtips just 4 m (13 ft) from the wall—going 250 km/h (155 mph). He completed the feat in just 44 seconds!

TUNNEL VISION?

Centenarian Pilot

At 102 years old, Jack Hemmings, a former Royal Air Force squadron leader, is the oldest person to fly a Spitfire! He took the controls and soared across London for 20 minutes on what he reported was a "bumpy" flight! The stunt raised money for the Mission Aviation Fellowship charity, which gives humanitarian aid by plane.

SOARING TO NEW HEIGHTS!

40 | CHAPTER 2: Above and Beyond

EAT OR COMPETE?

A unique way to be physically active is to involve food—and not as pre-performance fuel! Some of these just-for-fun competitions involve chasing, pushing, and even submerging the body in foodstuff to achieve victory—followed (we hope) by a quick hose down!

  SHARE

TOP PICK!

: Grappling in Gravy

In the quirky World Gravy Wrestling Championships, each round sees two competitors having a two-minute tussle in an inflatable wrestling ring flooded with gravy! The key to winning the championship is providing the best entertainment for the crowd. And although things do get a bit mucky, fire fighters are there to hose down the wrestlers after their bouts.

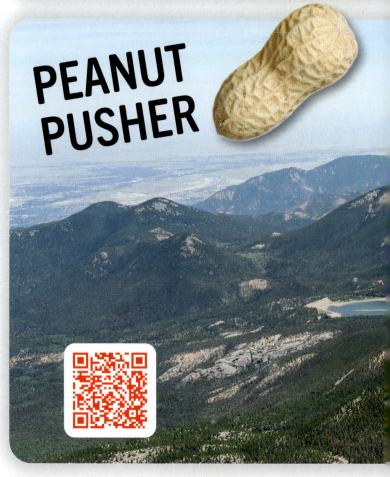

PEANUT PUSHER

CHAPTER 2: Above and Beyond | 41

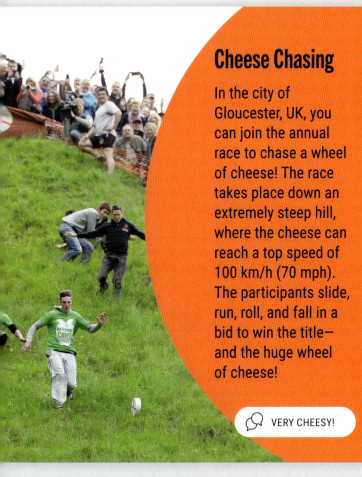

Cheese Chasing

In the city of Gloucester, UK, you can join the annual race to chase a wheel of cheese! The race takes place down an extremely steep hill, where the cheese can reach a top speed of 100 km/h (70 mph). The participants slide, run, roll, and fall in a bid to win the title—and the huge wheel of cheese!

💬 VERY CHEESY!

Pumpkins in a Pond

Oregon's Giant Pumpkin Regatta has competitors race across a pond in huge hollowed-out pumpkins. The vast vegetables can weigh up to 450 kg (1,000 lb), and bigger is better because they're steadier, so you're less likely to go splash! Dump trucks are used to remove the mountains of pumpkin innards!

With an unusual goal in mind, Bob Salem taped a spatula to his face and started pushing a peanut up a mountain with his new elongated nose! He covered 20 km (12 miles) in just seven days to reach the top of Pikes Peak, a summit in the Rocky Mountains. Over the week, he had to use more than 20 peanuts to complete the task!

MORE CRAZY CLIMBS ON PAGE 48! 👍

42 | CHAPTER 2: Above and Beyond

GROWN-UP GAMES

Games aren't just for kids! Grown-ups have found ways to use "kids' stuff" to have fun while competing. From chess—a game always popular with middle school kids—to back yard classic hula hooping, competitions get serious …

SHARE

Keepie Uppie Comp

In Spain's Balloon World Cup, the aim of the game is to stop the balloon from touching the floor. Matches last for two to five minutes on a court that resembles a furniture-filled lounge. The champions with the fewest balloon drops win serious prize money!

Checkmate or Knockout!

Chess boxing requires both brains and brawn! Two opponents first face each other for a three-minute session of speed chess, before putting on boxing gloves for a three-minute boxing round. They continue this way until one of them is defeated!

Tough Tug

In 2016, 4,672 people took part in the world's largest tug of war tournament! As part of a larger sporting event in Gujarat, India, people lined up to join the contest, which was organized to show that everyone can participate in sports to be fit and healthy.

ALTOGETHER NOW, PULL!

CHAPTER 2: Above and Beyond | 43

MORE ACROBATICS ON PAGE 49!

Hula Hooper

Israeli gymnast Linoy Ashram performed such a spectacular routine that it won her a gold medal in the Olympic Games. Her routine included throwing her plastic hoop high and catching it, spinning it around her wrists and ankles, and passing through the rolling hoop—all the while keeping her body and hoop under perfect control.

 GREAT FLEXIBILITY!

Sharp Shooters

Every year, in the village of Witcham, England, people take part in a contest to shoot dried peas at a putty-covered target from 3.5 m (12 ft) away. Participants can't use their own ammunition, but they can bring their own shooters—some even have laser guides for a more accurate shot!

| 44 | CHAPTER 2: Above and Beyond

JEOPARDOUS JUMPS

Whether jumping from a cliff or the stratosphere, using a pogo stick or a pole, extreme athletes look for extraordinary ways to test their physical strength and mental hardiness to take on some of the most breathtaking jumps the world has ever seen.

 SHARE

Space Jump

In 2012, daredevil Felix Baumgartner flew a helium-filled balloon to the stratosphere and skydived back to Earth in a specially made spacesuit. He reached a top speed of 1,357 km/h (843 mph) during free fall, breaking the speed of sound!

TOP PICK!

Pogopalooza

Extreme pogo athletes go to one place to show off their talents—the Pogopalooza World Championships in Pennsylvania. Pogo-mounted competitors attempt to jump over a high bar to beat the record of 3.6 m (12 ft) set by Dalton Smith in 2022.

ANOTHER DAREDEVIL JUMP ON PAGE 91!

CHAPTER 2: **Above and Beyond** | 45

Canal Vaulting

In the Netherlands, you can watch athletes take part in a contest where they sprint toward a canal, jump to cling onto a long pole standing in the water, and then drop to the other side of the canal as far as possible. This is "Fierljeppen," or canal vaulting, and the distance to beat is 17 m (56 ft)!

OFF A CLIFF!

Jump for success!

Extreme athlete Laso Schaller jumped off Cascata del Salto, a waterfall in Switzerland, to land 3.58 seconds later in the water below. The drop was a breathtaking 58.8 m (193 ft), and Laso reached 123 km/h (76 mph) before splashdown.

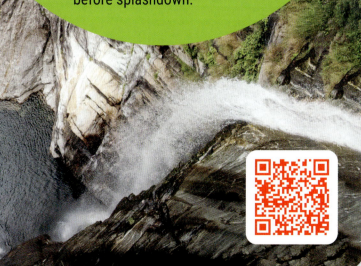

Ski Success

Imagine skiing down a long ramp, before flying through the air for over 7 seconds and landing 291 m (955 ft) away. That was the astonishing ski jump of Japanese Olympian Ryoyu Kobayashi in 2024, earning him a world record!

46 | CHAPTER 2: Above and Beyond

WHEELED WONDERS

Wins on wheels are often fast, sometimes dangerous, and always spectacular for the beholder! Thrill seekers and athletes use both their strong will and courage to steer their way to victory—whether they're racing or performing stunts.

FASTER, FASTER!

Scooter Circuits

The first-ever eSkootr Championship was held in London in 2022. The riders, with backgrounds in BMX, snowboarding, and speed skating, competed in short races on inner-city circuits. The specially designed electric scooters had a top speed of nearly 100 km/h (62 mph)!

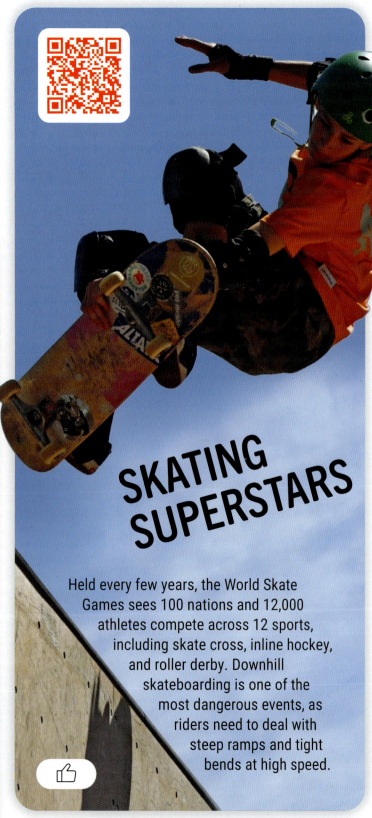

SKATING SUPERSTARS

Held every few years, the World Skate Games sees 100 nations and 12,000 athletes compete across 12 sports, including skate cross, inline hockey, and roller derby. Downhill skateboarding is one of the most dangerous events, as riders need to deal with steep ramps and tight bends at high speed.

MORE UNUSUAL SKATEBOARDING ON PAGE 58!

CHAPTER 2: Above and Beyond | 47

Superbike Stunt

Stunt rider Jonny Davies wore specially made titanium shoes so he could "ski" behind his superbike as it pulled him along at a speed of nearly 258 km/h (160 mph)! In addition to holding the motorbike steady, he then had to leap back onto it from behind while it was still moving.

TOP PICK!

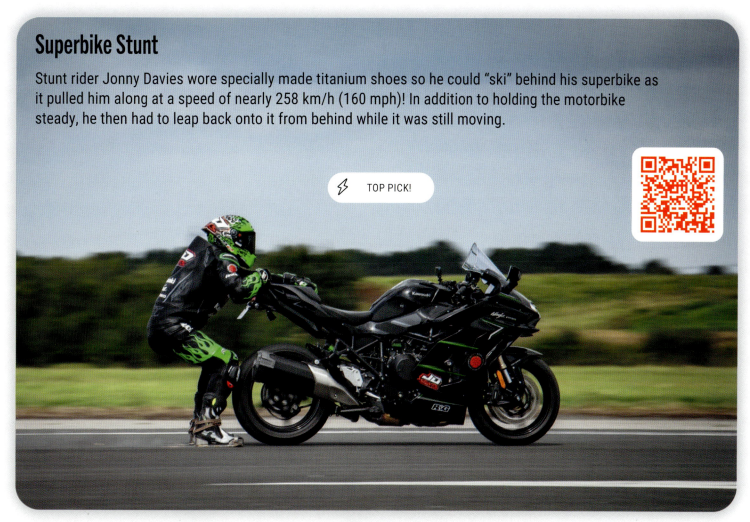

Mower Match

The British Lawnmower Championship doesn't involve making your grass look great. Instead, riders race around a track on mowers! Each mower has its blades removed and gears upgraded before completing 15–20 laps at a speedy-for-a-mower 29 km/h (18 mph)!

48 | CHAPTER 2: Above and Beyond

UP HIGH

You need a head for heights to perform some of the most dramatic deeds around. You could walk over a volcano, scale a building unaided, or twirl around a bar while hanging from a hot air balloon. Whatever you choose, just don't look down!

Scalding Steps

Could you overcome lava fountains and toxic fumes?

Walking a slackline seems tricky enough, but what if it was over an active volcano? Rafael Bridi and Alexander Schulz trained for three days a week, before taking on the precarious walk just 42 m (138 ft) above the crater of Mount Yasur in Vanuatu.

MORE VOLCANOES ON PAGE 72!

Everest Endurance

Sherpa guides use their expertise to help visitors reach the summit of the world's highest peaks. Sherpa Kami Rita has scaled Mount Everest—8,849 m (29,032 ft)—30 times, with one climb to the top taking just seven days!

CHAPTER 2: **Above and Beyond** | 49

Acrobatics at Altitude

Anna Cochrane's five-minute long trapeze act is impressive enough ... but she performed it hanging from a hot-air balloon! Anna trained every day leading up to the stunt, and when she dislocated a rib during the performance, she just carried on!

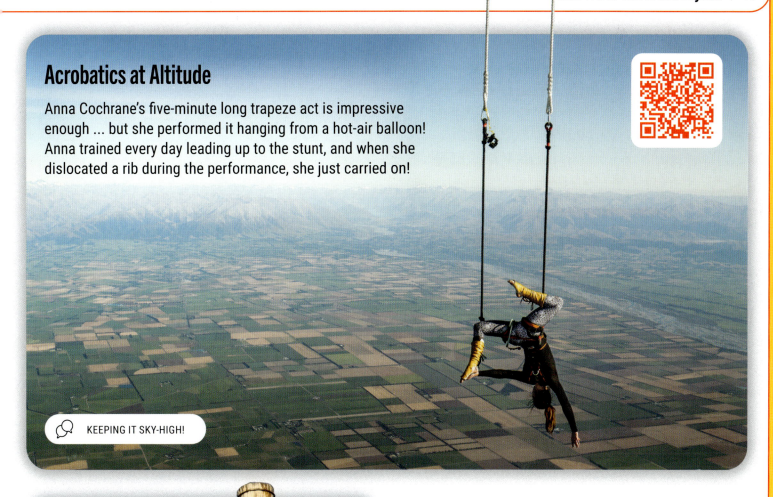

KEEPING IT SKY-HIGH!

Quick Clamber

In the Lumberjack World Championship, competitors race to the top of a 27-m (90-ft) pole, and drop back down again, as quickly as possible—in about 20 seconds! The only equipment used is a steel core climbing rope, spurs, gloves—and guts, of course!

Free Climb Feats

Nicknamed the French Spiderman, Alain Robert scales sky-high buildings around the world using just his bare chalked hands and climbing shoes. He's ascended the Eiffel Tower, the Empire State Building, and the Burj Khalifa—the world's tallest building.

DON'T LOOK DOWN!

50 | CHAPTER 2: Above and Beyond

WINS ON WATER

Water is challenging. It's ever-changing, immeasurably powerful, and often bitterly cold. But thrill seekers thrive on the rush of adrenaline as they harness its power and, for mere moments, work in harmony with it.

Extreme Experience

In 2024, Aniol Serrasolses set out on an awe-inspiring Arctic adventure. First he voyaged for 36 hours across the sea. Then he walked 11 km (7 mi) across snowy Svalbard. Finally, he paddled a kayak through rapids and ice tunnels, until he reached the final step—to drop 20 m (66 ft) down an icy waterfall into the freezing waters below. Brrrrr!

WHOPPING WAVE!

TOP PICK!

Boarding Below

If you think skateboarding on land is tricky, try it on water, towed behind a boat. This is wake skating. Champion Brian Grubb went one step further! He rode his board through the narrow caverns of an underground river in Indiana, US.

MORE FUN WITH ICE ON PAGE 65!

CHAPTER 2: **Above and Beyond** | 51

Kite-surfer Patri McLaughlin managed to surf a monster wave in Hawaii—more than 22 m (72 ft) in height—despite having surgery just four weeks before! Although he hadn't trained for it, Patri trusted his skills to move across the water—to him, it was too great an opportunity to miss.

Sensational Swimmer

Paralympian swimmer Ellie Simmonds has not only won five Olympic gold medals, but she also holds ten World Champion titles and seven European Champion titles. She began competing on the international stage at just 14 years old and broke many world records, including completing the 200 m freestyle in just 2 minutes, 44 seconds!

WHAT A MUDDERLY FANTASTIC FEAT!

Peaty Paddle

More than 150 people descend on a small town in Wales every summer to swim 60 m (200 ft) through a cold, muddy bog! Competitors wear flippers and a snorkel—their face must be in the water throughout the swim. The fastest time to complete this muddy marathon is 1 minute, 12 seconds!

 SHARE

CHAPTER 3
EXTRAORDINARY EVERYDAY

You don't have to look far for jaw-dropping feats—from breathtaking buildings to perilous pastimes!

Cool Clothes

Discover oversized T-shirts and crazy costumes.

PAGE 56

DID YOU KNOW?

There's actually a well-paid job diving for GOLF BALLS?!

Read all about it on page 69.

Performing Pets

Our best-loved companions show us who's smart.

PAGE 58

Ready, Set, Run!

Slither, gallop, or hop to the finish line with animals!

PAGE 54

Home Sweet Home

Choose your ideal home from this super selection!

PAGE 60

: Tough Trips

See where determination and guts can take you!

PAGE 62

: What a Job!

Discover the jobs that only a chosen few can do.

PAGE 68

: Spectacular Stays

From tree houses to cabins, these places are perfect!

PAGE 64

: Unforgettable Food

Disgusting or delicious? These food are unforgettable!

PAGE 70

: Colossal Collections

Get ready to be wowed by extraordinary sets of stuff!

PAGE 66

: Hazardous Hobbies

Experience some edge-of-your-seat hobbies!

PAGE 72

READY, SET, RUN!

From hamsters and snails to dogs and camels—animal racing is a popular event! Competitive owners try to find clever ways to encourage their animals to cross the finish line first!

Speedy Snails

In the World Snail Racing Championships, 200 snails try their luck at being the fastest to complete the 34-cm (13-in) course. The prize? A juicy lettuce leaf and gastropod glory! Snail racers often have brightly painted shells and turbo-sounding names, such as Speedy, Zoomer, and Uslime Bolt.

NOT SO FAST!

Robo-Racers

At the Al Shahaniya Track in Qatar, camels and their jockeys are racing superstars. The silk-clothed jockeys are remote-controlled robots, handled by trainers who are driving alongside the track. The trainers can pull on the reins and shout encouragement through a speaker. In clouds of dust, the camels charge forward at speeds of up to 64 km/h (40 mph) and complete each race in around 10 minutes.

CHAPTER 3: **Extraordinary Everyday** | 55

Clucking Competition

In a small village in Derbyshire, UK, an unusual race has taken place annually for the past 100 years—the World Hen Racing Championships. Around 50 hens compete on the 15-m (50-ft) racetrack, some crossing the finish line after just three or four seconds. The winning hen is given a bag of grain, and the owner is awarded a prized trophy.

WOW!

Ways to make your hen run faster include banging a tin, tapping a tuning fork, singing, or shaking a bucket of worms!

Canine Contestant

Run with *dogged* determination

The Hard Dog Race encourages dog owners and their loyal companions to work as a team. There are several races to choose from, the hardest being a 12-km (7.5-mi) run with 22 obstacles, including ramps, rivers, tunnels, and see-saws. What if a dog refuses to tackle an obstacle? It's a penalty of 30 squats for their human!

WOOF!

MORE DOGS ON PAGE 11!

COOL CLOTHES

Creative fashion designers have come up with some terrific clothing stunts—from the biggest to the smelliest—to put out a powerful message to the world about some important causes, while also having a bit of fun!

Titan T-shirt

A giant T-shirt was made in Romania out of 300,000 recycled plastic bottles! It took three weeks to collect the bottles, four weeks to make the T-shirt, and a whole day just to unfurl the finished garment. Even more amazingly, the T-shirt was later taken apart and made into 10,000 smaller items of clothing for underprivileged children.

Delicious Dress

A Swiss bakery went the extra mile to impress by making a wearable wedding dress out of cake! Supported by a metal frame, the cake dress weighed an astonishing 131 kg (289 lb)—the same as 58 bricks! The cake was beautifully decorated with hundreds of royal icing flowers, and was eventually enjoyed by the bakery's customers.

 THAT LOOKS YUMMY!

CHAPTER 3: Extraordinary Everyday | 57

Stinky Suit

Imagine wearing all the trash you've created in a whole month! That's what environmental activist Rob Green did to show just how much waste we make. By the end of the month he'd collected 60 kg (132 lb) of trash to pack into his clear plastic suit.

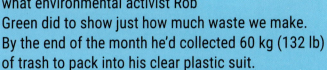

STINKY!

👍 💬 WHAT A WASTE!

👍

Crazy Costumes

What costume would you run in?

It seems that running a marathon and wearing a crazy costume go hand in hand. People dress up as animals, cartoon characters, and food—to have fun, stand out, and raise funds for charity. One year, a competitor dressed up as the London landmark Big Ben—only to discover he was too tall to cross the finish line!

PERFORMING PETS

Pets prove again and again that they are really quite intelligent—learning new physical and mental skills quickly and easily. But it seems there is one common theme … a tasty treat for a job well done!

   SHARE

Skateboarding Superstar

Meet the Go-Go-Goat!

When Happie the Goat seemed interested in wheels, her owner decided to teach her how to get on a skateboard. Motivated by food, Happie picked up the skill quickly and now jumps on the board independently. She can skate more than 35 m (115 ft) without stopping—although her steering needs a bit of work!

 NOW THAT'S IMPRESSIVE!

Feline Feat

Many people would believe that cats are too aloof to be trained. Well, not Alexis—this clever cat understands her owner's instructions to perform tricks such as high five, wave, and shake head. In fact—for a treat—Alexis can do 26 tricks, one after the other, in just 60 seconds!

 GIVE ME FIVE!

 WHO'S A CLEVER BOY!

Remem-bird

Apollo the parrot performs an amazing trick—when offered a pistachio or two! In just 3 minutes, he is able to name 12 objects, including book, socks, and plant. Apollo can now recognize a variety of words and objects, showing just how smart parrots can be.

CHAPTER 3: Extraordinary Everyday | 59

LOOK OUT!

Pigcasso

In South Africa, a rescue pig has astounded art lovers everywhere—by painting masterpieces! Pigcasso, as the rescue pig is known, was the first animal artist to host an exhibition, and her paintings have together sold for over $1 million. Although food rewards play a part, scientists believe she enjoys painting.

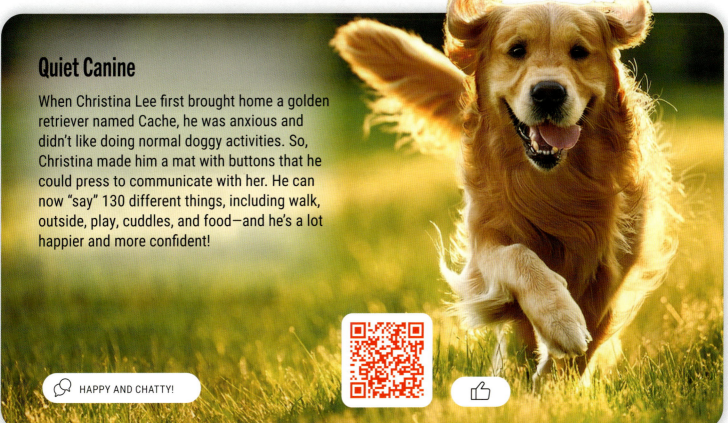

Quiet Canine

When Christina Lee first brought home a golden retriever named Cache, he was anxious and didn't like doing normal doggy activities. So, Christina made him a mat with buttons that he could press to communicate with her. He can now "say" 130 different things, including walk, outside, play, cuddles, and food—and he's a lot happier and more confident!

HAPPY AND CHATTY!

60 | CHAPTER 3: Extraordinary Everyday

HOME SWEET HOME

When you think of home, you might picture a house, apartment, or maybe a condo or houseboat. But what about more extreme abodes? If you've got a place to wash, eat, and sleep, there are so many options: big and small, new and recycled, up high and down low!

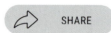 SHARE

Mirrored Mansion

An Estonian company called ÖÖD has designed a home that combines luxury and nature: the Golden House. This compact house has glowing golden-mirrored glass that reflects the natural surroundings as the seasons change. To prevent crashes, the house comes with UV stickers that birds, but not humans, can see.

Rocky Rooms

Coober Pedy, a town in Australia, is not only well known for mining beautiful opal gemstones, but also for its underground homes! In summer, temperatures reach 56 °C (133 °F), so the best place to be is in the cool subterranean sandstone settlements. And if you need more space, just dig yourself another room!

IT'S COOL HERE!

Aqua Abode

In 2023, Dr. Joseph Dituri—or Dr. Deep Sea— challenged himself to live in an undersea lodge in the Florida Keys for 100 days. The expedition wasn't just a crazy stunt, but a scientific experiment to learn how deep water and the extreme environment affected the human body. It's thought that underwater pressure may help prevent some age-related diseases.

IMAGINE LIVING BESIDE DEEP-SEA CREATURES!

SNAP!

CHAPTER 3: **Extraordinary Everyday** | 61

Cockpit Condo

Peek inside this high-flying house!

In 1999, Bruce Campbell set up an air-mazing home on his land in Oregon, US—in a Boeing 727. Costing just $100,000, the plane was brought over from Greece and fitted with a simple shower, sink, washing machine, fridge, and microwave. Bruce welcomes visitors to look around his home, and even hosts small concerts and events!

YOU'RE GROUNDED!

Incredible Carvings

Millions of people visit Cappadocia in Turkey each year, taking in the sights of the mushroom-shaped homes by hot-air balloon. The shapes were carved out of the pinkish stone by wind and rain over millions of years. The structures are no longer used as homes, but if you're feeling fairylike, you can stay in a unique cave hotel.

62 | CHAPTER 3: Extraordinary Everyday

TOUGH TRIPS

With steely determination, some people take tough trips covering vast distances and overcoming difficult hurdles. What keeps them going? Crowds of well-wishers and proving to themselves and everyone else that anything is possible, if you set your mind to it!

Woof and Walk

One day, a couple decided to take their dog on a long walk—1,014 km (630 mi) long, that is! The short legs of their Pomeranian mix, Arnie, couldn't manage every step from Somerset to Dorset, UK, so he caught a lift in a baby carrier!

HAVING A PAW-SOME TIME!

Balloon Record-breaker

The first nonstop flight around the world was achieved in a hot-air balloon called the *Breitling Orbiter 3*. Brian Jones and Bertrand Piccard flew from Switzerland to Egypt via India, China, and Japan, reaching a top speed of 190 km/h (180 mph). It took them just 20 days.

CHAPTER 3: Extraordinary Everyday | 63

African Adventure

In 2023, Russ Cook took on the awesome challenge of running through 16 countries from southern Africa to the northern tip, covering an astonishing 16,000 km (10,000 mi)—the same as 390 marathons. Due to a few incidents, including severe back pain, Russ took 100 days longer than planned, but he still managed it in an incredible 352 days.

TOP PICK!

Tandem Trip

Two cycling enthusiasts wanted to set a record—to be the fastest women to circumnavigate the globe on a tandem bike! They covered 29,000 km (18,000 mi) in 263 days, crossed 25 countries, and carried on despite monsoon rains and wildfire smoke!

LIFE IN THE FAST LANE!

ALTERNATIVE PEDAL-POWER ON PAGE 92!

SPECTACULAR STAYS

Many people seek something a little special when they stay away from home, be it a fancy tree house, cute cabin, or luxury hotel. But some places to stay go above and beyond the ordinary to give adventurous tourists the ultimate destination experience.

Salty Spa

Overlooking the stunning salt flats in Bolivia stands the Luna Salada hotel and spa. Everything inside the hotel is made from solid salt, including the walls, bed, tables, and chairs. But there is a downside for the hotel owners—salt is highly corrosive, so electrical wires need replacing often.

Spaceship Sleeper

The next best thing to visiting space is sleeping in a UFO-shaped cabin that sways in the trees 6 m (20 ft) off the ground! To reach this tree house cabin, you must deploy the retractable stairs—just like in the movies—and climb into the metal-clad structure. Everything inside is space themed for the ultimate out-of-this-world experience!

CHAPTER 3: **Extraordinary Everyday** | 65

IMAGINE A ROOM WITH *THIS* VIEW!

Reef Rooms

Sleeping in the big swim!

After a three-hour boat trip, tourists start one of the most dreamy stays imaginable—sleeping next to the majestic marine life of the Great Barrier Reef. The bedrooms are 3 m (10 ft) under the water, and each has a wall of windows looking out onto the coral reef and its fish, sharks, and turtles.

Snowy Snooze

It takes six weeks to rebuild Sweden's iconic Ice Hotel each year. Huge blocks of ice are taken from the frozen River Torne for the main structure. Then ice artists arrive to sculpt the ice gallery, creating sharks, trains, dinosaurs—whatever is needed! The hotel will stand for four months until spring arrives, and the ice begins to melt.

ICE-COOL ACCOMMODATION!

| 66 | CHAPTER 3: Extraordinary Everyday

COLOSSAL COLLECTIONS

Assembling a collection containing thousands of items takes dedication, time, and usually lots of space! And although gathering toys, everyday items, or memorabilia might seem unnecessary, these colossal collections show us an awesome snapshot of culture and life at a particular time.

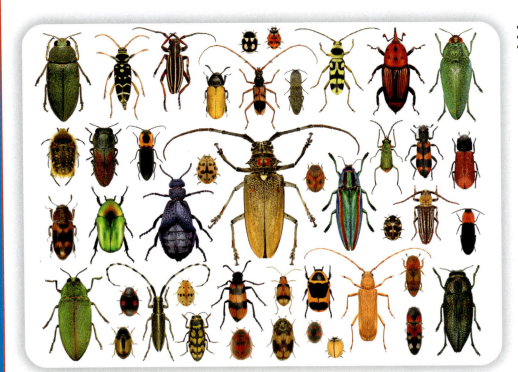

Big Batch of Bugs

How many different insect specimens could you collect in 60 years? 1.25 million, according to retired entomologists Charlie and Lois. Over their lifetime, they have visited 70 countries in the pursuit of new and exciting pieces. They've now donated their collection, worth £8 million ($10 million), to Arizona State University.

HEAPS OF HAMBURGERS!

Is he a food fan or a hungry hoarder?

A man from Florida, nicknamed "Hamburger Harry," has amassed more than 3,700 hamburger-related items. From clothing to cushions, he is surrounded by these fast-food friends. His prized possession is a custom-built Hamburger Harley motorbike with matching Hamburger Helmet!

LETTUCE KETCHUP WITH HARRY!

CHAPTER 3: **Extraordinary Everyday** | 67

Green Goddess

Artist and designer Elizabeth Sweetheart is known as the "Green Lady of Brooklyn" because, for the past 25 years, everything about her has been a shade of green! She has green clothes, hair, and nails. And although the walls are white, her home is filled with green chairs, tables, rugs, cushions, towels, plates, cups, and utensils. Even the soap is green!

Comic Collection

Creative and characterful, comics are great fun to read, but can you imagine owning more than 138,000 of them? Bob Bretall does. He was hooked at eight years old with his first comic, *The Amazing Spider-Man*. Bob's collection is still growing—by about 100 comics a month!

Lots of Lego

Since he was five years old, Miloš Křeček has collected Lego. He decided to open the "Museum of Bricks" in Prague to store and show off more than 6,750 Lego sets. He estimates that he's spent over 20,000 hours building. To achieve this, you'd need to build for eight hours a day, seven days a week, for nearly seven years!

68 | CHAPTER 3: Extraordinary Everyday

WHAT A JOB!

When you think of a future job, maybe a teacher, vet, or rock star come to mind. But there are some almost unimaginable jobs out there—sometimes dangerous, sometimes smelly, but always worthwhile.

SEE PAGE 48 FOR A DAREDEVIL VOLCANO STUNT!

Helicopter Heroes

Most overhead power lines can be reached using a ladder or truck. But in rugged, remote areas, helicopter lineworkers are the only option. As the helicopter riskily hovers close to the high-voltage line, quick-thinking lineworkers balance on a platform to inspect issues and fix faults—next to a mega 110,000 volts.

Samurai Street Cleaners

On the streets of Tokyo, Japan, a group of unusually dressed litter pickers are getting noticed: Samurai Street Cleaners! Dressed in black-and-white tunics, with waste baskets on their backs, the Eco-Samurai wield their swords to gracefully clean up the streets, highlighting how much trash is discarded in the wrong place.

CHAPTER 3: **Extraordinary Everyday** | 69

Hot, Hot, Hot!

Volcanologists are daring detectives, constantly looking at how a volcano behaves so they can predict what it might do next—namely how and why a volcano erupts. This important scientific work can stop towns, homes, and lives being destroyed by an unexpected eruption.

WHAT A LAVA-LY JOB!

Diving for Golf Balls

Professional divers are used to collect golf balls from the bottom of rivers, ponds, and lakes. The water is often cold, dark, and muddy as the diver gropes around for the lost balls. In winter, a diver might even have to smash through ice. Amazingly, a diver can collect a million lost golf balls each year!

Feeding a Zoo

Zoo chefs have trickier customers than you might think! For animals from leafcutter ants to mighty elephants, zoo chefs must prepare meals that contain the right food, in the right amount, and which are given at the right time. A manatee needs to eat about 100 lettuces every day, but a python needs just one meaty meal every few weeks!

CHOMP, CHOMP!

TOP PICK!

UNFORGETTABLE FOOD

What makes a meal memorable? Maybe it's where you ate or being adventurous about what you tried, or maybe it's when the food was something ordinary turned into something extraordinary! Whatever it is, these chefs try hard to make the menu both delicious and momentous.

Ancient Eggs

Chinese "century eggs" aren't 100 years old—although they look it! Traditional makers cover raw eggs in a paste of tea, quicklime, salt, and ash, before storing them in a bag for about 30 days. The final product—turning the egg yellow, black, and brown—is considered to be a great delicacy and is mainly eaten on special occasions.

FOR FUNNY FOOD FESTIVALS, SEE PAGE 16!

Space Snacks

Food in space was once thought to be mainly freeze-dried and dull. But did you know, astronauts now enjoy pizza night? With the bases and toppings provided, the astronauts simply design their perfect pizza. Easy, right? Except everything floats, so they need to be quick not to lose a slice of pepperoni or two!

CHAPTER 3: Extraordinary Everyday | 71

Monster Veggies

Many towns host giant vegetable championships, where growers showcase their truly monstrous veggies! After the winning vegetable has been chosen, the growers remove the seeds and get cooking. Sauces and chutneys are popular. One year, a grower sent a colossal cabbage to a school, where it was studied before feeding more than 1,000 students!

Bug Burgers

Could you try this creepy crawly cuisine?

Insects are eaten by two billion people around the world—a quarter of the Earth's population. Mealworms, crickets, and locusts are particularly popular; they are made into burgers, chips, and pasta. They're plentiful, high in protein, and low in fat—and may be on many menus in the future!

SHARE

HAZARDOUS HOBBIES

 SHARE

Thrill seekers often hunt for hobbies that make their hearts beat a little faster. Armed with courage and curiosity, they discover the most extreme activities to fill their free time—pushing themselves to the ultimate limit.

Volcano Sledding

The slopes of Cerro Negro volcano in Nicaragua are coated in layers of ash and sand—perfect for a spot of seriously steep sledding. It takes thrill seekers an hour to climb to the top of the boarding path, about 460 m (1,500 ft) up. There, they mount a board made of plywood and metal, hold on tight to the ropes, and slide down at up to 95 km/h (60 mph) in just two minutes!

STORM CHASING

Subzero Sprint

Marathon runners on top of the world!!

Since 2003, nearly 600 people from 54 countries have taken part in the North Pole Marathon. It takes place on the floating ice of the Arctic Ocean with marshals scanning the landscape for polar bears. There's also a marathon in Antarctica for those competitors who can't get enough of cold weather running!

CHAPTER 3: **Extraordinary Everyday** | 73

With 1,200 storms hitting the US every year, it's not surprising that getting close to destructive tornadoes is a welcome challenge for thrill seekers. The aim is to be in the right place at the right time, experiencing the storm's power first-hand, while recording vital data that might one day help scientists to understand more.

Courageous Cowgirl

Imagine performing gymnastics in front of huge crowds, while on the back of a galloping horse! This is Bella da Costa's dream-come-true hobby. And when she's not performing stunts at rodeos—such as the extremely dangerous splits on horseback—Bella teaches trick-riding, helping kids to master extreme stunts.

WOULD YOU DARE TO DO THIS?

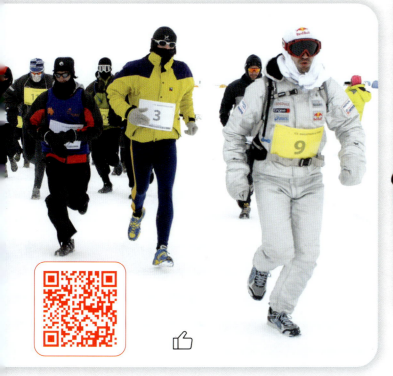

CHAPTER 4
TOP TECH

When we join forces with technology—and use a little imagination—the sky's the limit with what we can achieve!

Awe-inspiring Inventions
Get ready to be amazed by these techy ideas.
PAGE 78

DID YOU KNOW? There's a gigantic crane that can lift the weight of 1,200 elephants! Read all about it on page 84.

Mini Mechanics
Discover miniature motorbikes and medical marvels.
PAGE 80

Let's Go Fast!
These powerful machines are streamlined and speedy!
PAGE 76

Robots Assemble
Working together, robots can achieve great things.
PAGE 82

Mighty Machines

Discover mega and mighty machines.
PAGE 84

Long and Strong

Find out which "long" records have been smashed!
PAGE 90

Inspiring Inventions

Learn how some machines came from a simple idea.
PAGE 86

People Power

Learn all about human-powered technology.
PAGE 92

Helping Hand

Explore how tech helps people in their day-to-day lives.
PAGE 88

Ridiculous Rides

Whether made from wood or blocks, weird cars are cool!
PAGE 94

CHAPTER 4: Top Tech

LET'S GO FAST!

Engineers combine the most efficient sources of power with lightweight, streamlined designs to push their machines to the limits.

  SHARE

Monster Move

Joe Sylvester has set many records in his *Bad Habit* monster truck, including flooring the foot pedal until his beast of a vehicle reached a whopping 163 km/h (101 mph). Joe enjoys the thrill of pushing himself and his monster machine to the limit, all in the name of entertainment.

Drone Dash

If at first you don't succeed, try, try, try again. This is the motto father-and-son duo Mike and Luke Bell lived by when their speed-drone prototype kept catching fire! Many attempts later, they unveiled *Peregreen 2*, built with 3D-printed parts and an ultra-light frame. And when test day came, *Peregreen 2* reached a top speed of 480 km/h (298 mph)!

Fast F1

Formula 1 cars are phenomenally fast! They can accelerate from 0 to 96 km/h (60 mph) in just 2.6 seconds. Along a racetrack straight, speeds of 354 km/h (220 mph) are not uncommon. And at the 2020 Italian Grand Prix in Monza, Lewis Hamilton completed the fastest ever lap in Formula 1 history—with an average speed of 264 km/h (164 mph)!

CHAPTER 4: **Top Tech** | 77

TURBO-CHARGED YACHT!

Gusty Thrust

On board the land yacht *Horonuku*, Glenn Ashby smashed the overland speed record by reaching 222.4 km/h (138.1 mph)—powered only by wind! The craft was 14 m (46 ft) long and used an 11-m (36-ft) rigid wing as a sail to achieve maximum thrust.

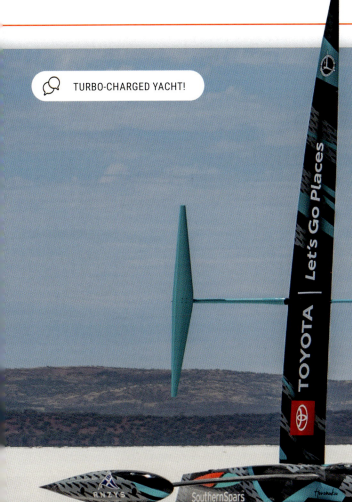

SPEED TO SUCCEED!

MORE CARS ON PAGE 94!

CHAPTER 4: Top Tech

AWE-INSPIRING INVENTIONS

Inventors are inspired by movies, comic book heroes, and natural displays of wonder, but some tech ideas are beyond anything most people could imagine.

 SHARE

Rescue Jet Pack
Superhero rescue at the ready!

British inventor Richard Browning has developed a jet pack that is being tested by medical, rescue, and military teams to get to hard-to-reach places quickly. Each jet pack has a large engine on the back and thrusters on the wearer's arms, enabling it to travel at 136 km/h (85 mph).

UP AND AWAY!

Cortex Chip

A man who is quadriplegic (affected by paralysis in all four limbs) has been able to use his hand to play online chess, thanks to an implant in his brain. The chip was inserted into Noland Arbaugh's left motor cortex and uses 16 electrodes to control the movement of his right hand. Before this, Noland played chess using a mouth-controlled joystick.

CHECKMATE!

CHAPTER 4: Top Tech | 79

MOVE OUT OF MY WAY!

Dream Come True

British engineer Matt Denton has wanted to build a walking robot ever since he saw *Star Wars* when he was eight years old. And now he's done it with a six-legged robot that you can ride inside! The giant hexapod called Mantis measures nearly 3 m (9 ft) by 5 m (16 ft), and its legs are controlled by a computer.

Brain Power

A bionic arm has been developed that is so sensitive, it can respond to the power of thought and enable the user to pick up small objects like coins. In tests, the prosthetic was permanently attached to the user's arm bone. Electrodes implanted into the nerves and muscles sent signals to the robotic arm to control it.

MINI MECHANICS

Some machines are built to be super small. Why? They're often less expensive to make, more of a challenge to build, and can get to hard-to-reach areas more easily.

  SHARE

SPACE DRONE

Exploring Mars by air!

NASA has launched a tiny helicopter … on Mars! During its first flight of less than a minute, it hovered 3 m (10 ft) above the planet's surface, before landing safely. It had to turn its rotor blades 2,500 times a minute to stay airborne in such a thin atmosphere. The Martian mini-marvel was named *Ingenuity*.

OUT OF THIS WORLD!

Mini Moto

Around the world, there are mini motorbike championships—with adult riders doing the racing! These 30-kg (66-lb) kid-sized bikes have just 13 horsepower, compared to MotoGP's 260 hp. What they lack in power, they make up for in spectacle as skilled riders try to keep their limbs tucked in and avoid crashing!

SHARE

Remote-controlled Pill

Go to the doctor's with a stomach problem and you may be asked to swallow a teeny robot! This technology allows a doctor to explore the digestive system using a handheld controller—just like in a video game. The robot's camera sends a live feed to a computer so the doctor can see any issues. The best part? Patients can't feel a thing!

CHAPTER 4: Top Tech | 81

Condensed Copter

Weighing just 70 kg (154 lb), the small GEN H4 helicopter can stay airborne for 30 minutes and reach a top speed of 50 km/h (30 mph). It has two rotors that turn in opposite directions to keep the helicopter stable.

Micro Machines

The Peel P50 car was designed in the 1960s for just one adult and a bag. It measures just 1.4 m (4.5 ft) long and weighs less than an adult man, which is important! In order to reverse the car, the driver must get out and physically turn the car around using a handle!

IN A TIGHT SPOT!

82 | CHAPTER 4: Top Tech

ROBOTS ASSEMBLE

What's more impressive than a smart robot? Lots of smart robots! From cheerleading squads to display drones, robots—sometimes up to thousands at a time—work together to both help and entertain us.

Dancing Dobis

Imagine a robot dancing—and then multiply that by 1,069! That's the number of robots which all danced at exactly the same time to break a world record. As well as dancing, the Dobi robots can sing, kick a ball, talk, and do tai chi moves!

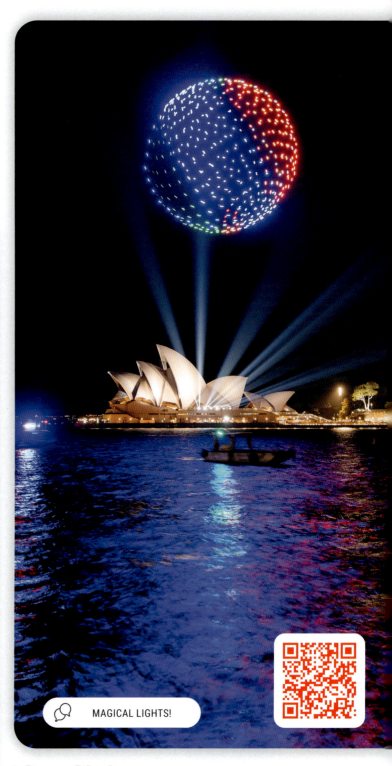

MAGICAL LIGHTS!

Drone Display

The sky's the limit!

Forget fireworks—a drone show to light up the dark sky is the way forward! Every year, above Sydney Harbour, there is a spectacular light-and-sound show, using more than 1,000 drones. Recent shows have featured planets in the Solar System and natural wonders—all made from light-up drones!

CHAPTER 4: **Top Tech** | 83

Robot Cheerleaders

If you can't fill a stadium with cheering fans, what do you do to boost the morale of your team? Bring in a robot cheerleading squad, of course! More than 40 robots, some resembling humans and some resembling dogs, danced to the anthem of the Japanese baseball team, Fukuoka SoftBank Hawks, in a game against the Rakuten Eagles. Did the support help? Yes! The home team won 4–3!

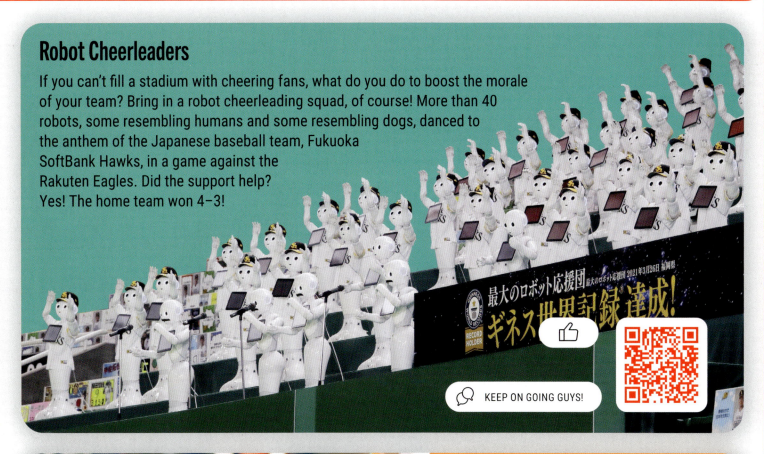

KEEP ON GOING GUYS!

Copious Cars

The biggest car factory in the world is the Wolfsburg Volkswagen Factory in Germany. It covers an enormous 6.5 sq km (2.5 sq mi)! It's so big that there are 6,000 bicycles dotted around for employees to get from one area to another. The factory uses 4,200 robot arms to produce 800,000 cars a year—that's one every 16 seconds!

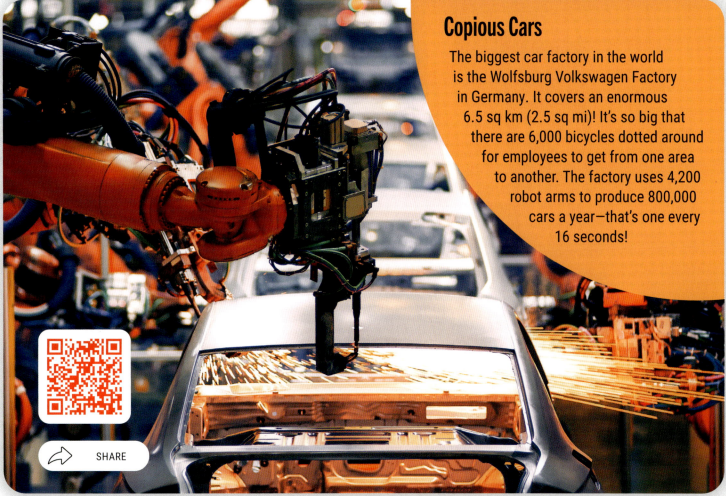

SHARE

84 | CHAPTER 4: Top Tech

MIGHTY MACHINES

The most massive machines in the world are usually built for construction sites to move mega amounts of material. But some are also built just for fun, to test the limits of what humans can create with modern technology.

Enormous Excavator

The Bagger 293 is a 14,000-tonne (15,432-ton) bucket-wheel excavator used to mine coal from the ground. As the wheel turns, 18 buckets each dig out 15 m³ (530 ft³) of material per scoop, and then dump it onto a conveyor belt to be taken away. This mega machine can move 200,000 tonnes (220,462 tons) of earth every day.

WOW, THAT'S MEGA!

Colossal Crane

The SK6000 is the world's strongest land-based crane. With a 4,200-tonne (4,630-ton) counterweight, it can lift huge loads—the same as 1,200 elephants! It can be used for many projects, such as placing wind turbines in one piece and constructing offshore oil platforms.

CHAPTER 4: Top Tech | 85

MEGA MOTORBIKE

As tall as a giraffe, as heavy as an elephant!
Motorbike-mad Fabio Reggiani made the world's tallest motorbike—and it actually works! It stands at more than 5 m (16 ft) tall, which is six times bigger than a normal motorbike. It took a team of eight people to build the bike in just six months, with almost every piece needing to be handmade. The wheels came from an excavator!

Titanic Tetrapod

This giant, spider-like machine is the world's largest tetrapod exoskeleton! The frame measures 5×5 m (16×16 ft). Four hydraulic legs are connected to a sensitive control panel, enabling them to move in unison with the pilot's movements.

CHAPTER 4: Top Tech

INSPIRING INVENTIONS

 SHARE

Advancing technology has enabled humans to achieve feats beyond their wildest dreams, but what inspiring inventions may you never have imagined in the first place?

Robot Parkour

Boston Dynamics has developed a humanoid robot, called Atlas, capable of adjusting its movements so rapidly that it can take part in parkour. The robot can jump, balance, and navigate different surface angles to get around a course. The team hopes Atlas will be a step forward in the technology of robotic mobility.

Robo Suit

Simon Kindleysides is paralyzed, but he can walk 10,000 steps a day using a robotic exoskeleton suit! Controlled by his watch, the suit is designed to replicate how a human walks—it can even manage stairs. The only drawback is the suit can't yet walk quickly, meaning it takes Simon 48 minutes to walk 1.6 km (1 mi).

CHAPTER 4: Top Tech | 87

PAMPERED PETS

Drying a dog after a wet walk can be an unpleasant task—step into the PEPE Pet Dry Room! Although it looks a bit like a giant microwave, it was developed to give your pampered pooch a stress-free blow-dry! It's quiet and comfortable, and it dries dogs in under half an hour!

NO MORE WET PETS!

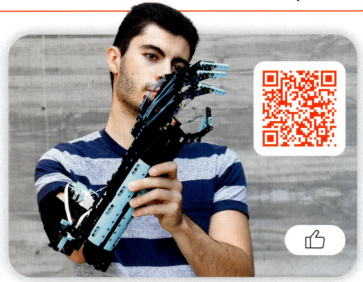

Lego Limb

David Aguilar was only nine years old when he built his first prosthetic arm—named Mark I—out of Lego blocks. Fourteen years later, he became the proud inventor of Mark V, a motorized Lego arm with five fingers that responds to sensors on his arm. David promotes building prostheses out of Lego because the blocks are affordable and readily available.

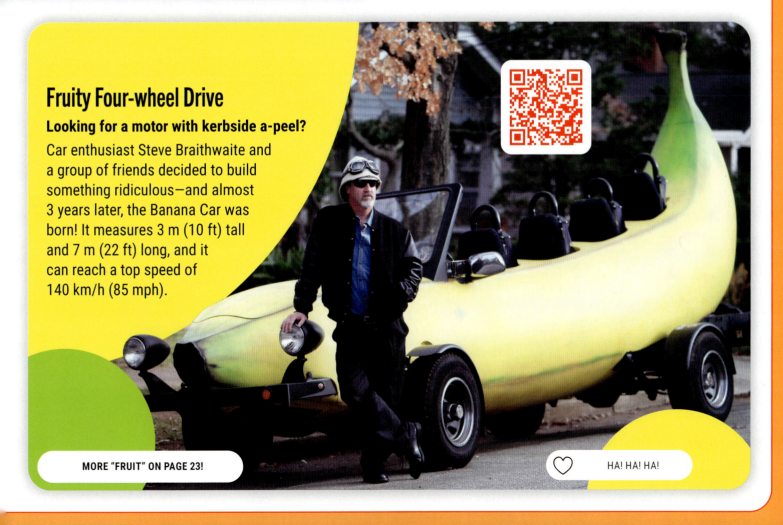

Fruity Four-wheel Drive

Looking for a motor with kerbside a-peel?

Car enthusiast Steve Braithwaite and a group of friends decided to build something ridiculous—and almost 3 years later, the Banana Car was born! It measures 3 m (10 ft) tall and 7 m (22 ft) long, and it can reach a top speed of 140 km/h (85 mph).

MORE "FRUIT" ON PAGE 23!

HA! HA! HA!

88 | CHAPTER 4: Top Tech

HELPING HAND

The power and intelligence of robots can be used to give humans an efficient helping hand with jobs that are dangerous, boring, or too challenging—from working in hot kitchens to picking fresh produce.

SHARE

Helpful Harvester

Robots are being developed to harvest delicate fruit and vegetables. Each robot can easily judge whether the fruit is ripe enough, pick it by the stalk, test it for disease, and fill trays until they reach the required weight.

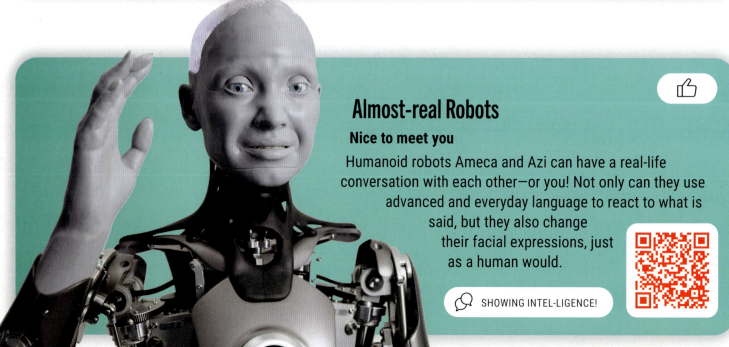

Almost-real Robots

Nice to meet you

Humanoid robots Ameca and Azi can have a real-life conversation with each other—or you! Not only can they use advanced and everyday language to react to what is said, but they also change their facial expressions, just as a human would.

SHOWING INTEL-LIGENCE!

CHAPTER 4: **Top Tech** | 89

Botanical Bot

In 2021, a robot that looked like a sloth lived among the trees of Atlanta Botanical Gardens! For 13 months, this 1-m (3-ft) bot monitored the surrounding environment, collecting data on pollution and air temperature. Powered by solar energy, it would move along its cable into a sunny spot to recharge. Like a real sloth (below), it conserved energy by moving very slowly.

Cyborg Chef

A fast-food restaurant in California uses robots to cook all the food. The robot arm "Flippy" can make 100 kg (250 lb) of fries or 100 meat patties in just one hour, and it never needs a break or a day off! However, human chefs are still needed to add toppings and build the burgers.

MMM, TASTY!

MORE ROBOTS ON PAGE 25!

CHAPTER 4: Top Tech

LONG AND STRONG

The world of fantastic feats includes some of the "longest" achievements around, from supersize vehicles to the impressive distances covered by both ordinary and extraordinary technology!

Bulky Bicycle

A team of 10 engineering enthusiasts from the Netherlands built a pedal-powered bicycle that measured 55 m (180 ft) long! It consisted of just two wheels, a *looooong* steel frame, and handlebars. The determined designers rode the record-breaking bike for 100 m (328 ft) to the applause of onlookers!

Paper Plane

Imagine using a piece of paper and some tape to make a plane that flies 77 m (253 ft)! That was the record-breaking achievement of Kim Kyu Tae from South Korea. The design remains a closely guarded secret, with Kim only revealing that the choice of paper was critical to its success.

SOARING SUCCESS!

MORE MOTORBIKES ON PAGE 85!

CHAPTER 4: **Top Tech** | 91

Toy Track

Former NASA engineer Mark Rober built a track for toy cars that twisted and turned for more than 800 m (2,640 ft) around a warehouse. The track went up and down staircases, through walls, and powered along lengthy straights using 75 "speed booster" mechanisms.

Duo Jump

Australian stunt performers Jake Bennett and Mel Eckert wanted to break a world record ... together! They mounted their motorbike for an almighty jump and flew 37 m (121 ft) through the air. Jake rehearsed the stunt wearing a weighted vest to mimic the load of two people.

WOW!

The longest motorbike jump by a single rider was set in 2012. US stunt performer Alex Harvill jumped an incredible 129.54 m (425 ft)!

PEOPLE POWER

To master human-powered machines, you need physical strength, skilled design, and lots of spirit! These people-powered vehicles are seen in both silly races and serious competitions as people make it their mission to "fly" through the air and water.

  SHARE

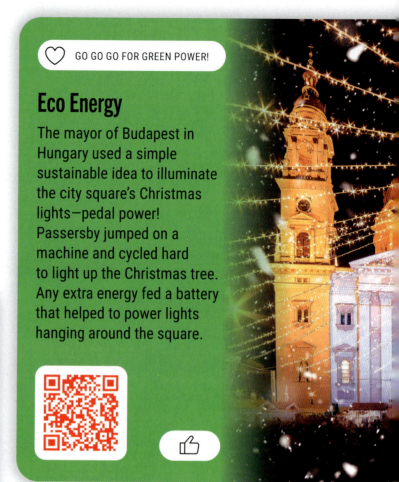

GO GO GO FOR GREEN POWER!

Eco Energy

The mayor of Budapest in Hungary used a simple sustainable idea to illuminate the city square's Christmas lights—pedal power! Passersby jumped on a machine and cycled hard to light up the Christmas tree. Any extra energy fed a battery that helped to power lights hanging around the square.

Pedal-powered Pods

If your legs are feeling strong, you might have a chance of winning a Schweeb race—where two opponents cycle their pods along a 200-m (656-ft) monorail racetrack at a speed of up to 50 km/h (30 mph). The record time to complete the three-lap race is just 1 minute, 3 seconds!

Bike Flight

A bicycle-powered helicopter was able to stay in the air for 64 seconds! The Atlas helicopter, built by students at the University of Toronto, used an ultra-light frame with giant rotors at each corner and a bicycle in the middle.

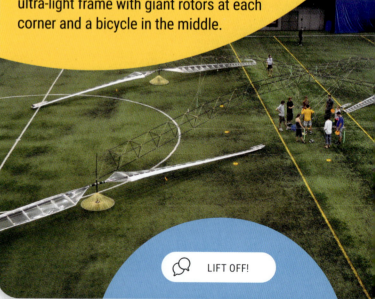

LIFT OFF!

CHAPTER 4: Top Tech | 93

Special Submarines

The International Human-Powered Submarine Race sees students design, build, and race their subs over a two-week period. A bike mechanism powers the back propeller, which turns and pushes the sub forward. To win the competition, students must steer around a slalom course and deal with any underwater challenges they encounter.

Anything Goes!

Competitors enter the Red Bull Flugtag with hand-built, human-powered flying machines! The aim of the competition is to "fly" as far as possible once pushed off an 8-m (27-ft) flight deck. The distance to beat is 78.5 m (257 ft) by the "Chicken Whisperers" team. Other wacky designs have included dragons, pug dogs, toilet rolls, and sausages!

94 | CHAPTER 4: Top Tech

RIDICULOUS RIDES

Many hobbyists and engineers thrive on the challenge of using unusual materials to create eye-catching builds, especially when it comes to developing unique vehicles that cause a stir!

CRAZY CARS

Sudha Cars Museum in India hosts the largest collection of wacky vehicles. The museum founder and car transformer Kanyaboyina Sudhakar has built full-sized cars that look like shoes, balls, computers, and even a chessboard! It takes him six to twelve months to make each one, and he hopes to eventually create 100 crazy cars!

Wooden Wagon

French carpenter Michel Robillard crafted a drivable car out of wood! It took him five years and an astonishing 5,000 hours to complete the project. The car can travel at 80 km/h (50 mph), but it's not legally allowed on the road. At a 2023 auction, Michel's masterpiece was sold for £175,000 ($223,000).

💬 WOOD YOU BELIEVE IT!

CHAPTER 4: **Top Tech** | 95

Block Bugatti

The creative team at Lego love a challenge. They took engineering a brick Bugatti in their stride—even though it needed to be life-sized and drivable! It took more than 1 million pieces and 13,500 hours to complete the super car, which was powered with 2,000 Lego motors!

Jaw-dropping Dodgems

Imagine driving along a road in California and seeing ten DODGEM cars cruising alongside you. You might wonder if they belong in a fairground. And, yes, they do! But Tom Wright had the fun idea—and skill—to convert them. It took him a year to restore the set, giving them new frames and engines. Each car can reach a speed of 100 km/h (60 mph)!

SHARE

INDEX

air guitar 34–5
altitude-based activities 48–9
animals 14, 35, 60, 62, 69, 73, 89
   in art 8–9
   drying 86–7
   festivals 10–11
   performing 58–9
   races 54–5
art 8–9, 14–15, 20–5
Artificial Intelligence 25

ball games 30–1
bikes 5, 47, 80–1, 85, 90–3
bionics 79
bugs 14, 66, 71

cake 22, 56
cars 9, 18–19
   Formula 1 76–77
   tiny 81
   toy 25, 91
   unusual 87, 94–95
car factory 83

clothing 12–13, 56–7, 57
collections 66–7

dance 32–3, 82
dinosaurs 14
dogs 11, 59, 62, 86–7

elephants 8–9, 76

festivals 10–13, 16–17
flight 38–9, 61–2, 68, 76, 78, 80–2, 90, 92–3

food 56, 69, 70–1, 89
   art 22–3
   competitions 40–1
   festivals 16–17
football 31
helicopter 38, 68, 80, 81, 92
homes 60–1
hotels 64–5

ice 14, 18–19, 50, 65, 69, 72
insects 14, 66, 71
inventions 74–5, 78–9, 86–7

jobs, tough 68–9

Lego 67, 87, 95

machines 76–95
marathon 63, 57, 72
medicine 80
mega art 8–9
monster truck 76
motorbikes 47, 66, 80, 85, 91
music 18–19, 26–7

origami 15

prosthetics 79, 87
pumpkins 16–17, 23, 41, 71

quadball 31

robots 24–5, 54, 74–5, 79, 82–3, 86, 88–9
Rubik's Cube 36

safety issues 4, 5
skydive 38, 44
space 44, 70
speed 36–7, 76–7
sport 28–31, 34–7, 40–7, 69, 72–3, 83
storm chasing 72–3
submarine 93

technology 24–5, 76–95
toy cars 25, 91

Vikings 12
volcanoes 48, 68–9, 72

water sports 50–1